UNEXPLAINED
MYSTERIES OF
WORLD WAR II

UNEXPLAINED
MYSTERIES OF
WORLD WAR II

ROBERT JACKSON

THE APPLE PRESS

A QUINTET BOOK

Published by The Apple Press
6 Blundell Street
London N7 9BH

ISBN 1-85076-297-X

This book was designed and produced by
Quintet Publishing Limited
6 Blundell Street
London N7 9BH

Creative Director: Terry Jeavons
Designers: Chris Dymond, Peter Radcliffe
Project Editor: Lindsay Porter
Editor: Michael Bennie
Picture Researcher: Liz Eddison
Illustrations: Danny McBride, Pilot Press

Typeset in Great Britain by
Central Southern Typesetters, Eastbourne
Manufactured in Hong Kong by
Regent Publishing Services Limited
Printed in Hong Kong by
C & C Offset Printing Co., Ltd.

Contents

'Lady Be Good' – The Lost Liberator

Four hundred and forty miles south of Benghazi, in the heart of the torrid, featureless wasteland that makes up the Libyan Desert, there lies the crumpled wreck of a wartime bomber.

It is a Consolidated B-24 Liberator. On its nose it bears the number 64 and the sun-faded name 'Lady be Good'. One day in April, 1943, it took off from the airfield at Soluk, on the coastal strip south of Benghazi, to attack enemy targets in Italy – and was not seen again for more than 16 years.

Then, in the late summer of 1959, reports began to reach the United States Air Force (USAF) head-quarters at Wheelus Field, Libya, that an oil sur-vey expedition had sighted the wreck of a large aircraft of World War Two vintage lying in the desert. A search crew was sent out in a C-47 trans-port with orders to land nearby and investigate the wreckage. They went with the grim knowledge that inside the wreck they might find the remains of the crew members who had disappeared with the bomber all those years ago.

The C-47 touched down safely on gravelly ground and the air force investigators disembarked into blistering heat and total silence. They quickly identified the crashed aircraft as a Liberator, and as they walked towards the wreckage an amazing sight met their eyes. There was no sign of corrosion on the bomber's metalwork. The dry, furnace-like desert air had preserved it perfectly. It was as though the Liberator had been plucked out of time and deposited there only the day before.

It lay on its belly, its right wing raised slightly, its left wing crumpled in the sand. The rear fusel-age and tail unit had broken away and was lying off to one side at an angle. One of its Twin Wasp

radial engines had been torn off. The starboard landing gear had dropped from its well and the tyre was still inflated.

Scattered debris lay littered around it: oxygen bottles, steel helmets, first-aid boxes, ammunition belts and items of flying clothing. Cautiously, the investigators peered inside the fuselage. Thank-fully, they found no mummified crew remains. The interior was completely deserted.

Sweltering in the blistering heat, they clambered inside to make a full search. They tested the radio receiver, and found that it was still in working order. They discovered vacuum flasks with warm coffee inside them, and it was still drinkable.

A B O V E The crumbled wreckage of 'Lady be Good' as it was found 17 years after the crash.

6

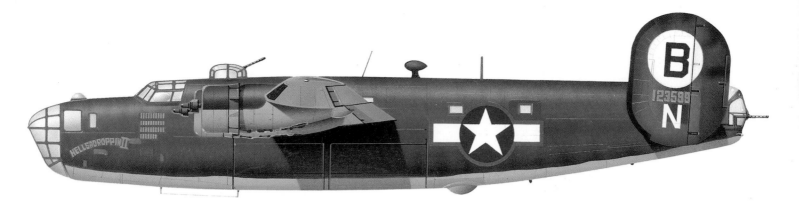

The fuel in the Liberator's tanks, the investigators found, was practically exhausted. Three of the four engines must have stopped in flight, because the propeller blades were 'feathered' – turned edge-on to the airflow to cut down drag. The fourth engine appeared to have still been working at the time of the crash.

By now it was clear that the crew had taken to their parachutes. In its last moments the bomber had been flying on automatic pilot, presumably to keep it steady while the crew abandoned ship.

One question was uppermost in everyone's mind. The Liberator showed no sign of having suffered battle damage, and the crew had obviously abandoned it as it ran out of fuel. But what was it doing here, hundreds of miles from where it ought to have been?

Back at Wheelus Field, the investigators compiled their report on what they had found at the crash site and forwarded it to Washington. From wartime USAF records, details of the bomber and its crew – and of their last flight – were unearthed.

ABOVE A B–24 Liberator, like the 'Lady be Good' which crashed into the Libyan desert.

BELOW A USAF C-47, like this one, was sent out to investigate the wreck of the lost Liberator.

B-24 Liberator No. 64 and its crew, captained by First Lieutenant William J. Hatton of New York, first came together in March, 1943 at Morrison Air Force Base, Florida. The other crew members were Second Lieutenant Robert F. Toner of North Attleboro, Massachusetts, Second Lieutenant David P. Hays of Lee's Summit, Montana, Second Lieutenant John S. Woravka of Cleveland, Ohio, Technical Sergeant Harold S. Ripslinger of Saginaw, Michigan, Technical Sergeant Robert E. Lamotte of Lake Linden, Michigan, Staff Sergeant Guy E. Shelley of New Cumberland, Pennsylvania, Staff Sergeant Vernon L. Moore of New Boston, Ohio, and Staff Sergeant Samuel R. Adams of Eureka, Illinois.

It was they who chose the name 'Lady Be Good' for their Liberator, and they painted it on the nose themselves. Almost immediately they were assigned to overseas duty, and departed on the long transatlantic flight to join the 376th Bomb Group at Soluk, Libya.

On 4 April, 1943, Hatton and his crew were briefed on their first combat mission. Theirs would be one of 25 B-24s taking part in an attack on enemy airfields around Naples, 750 miles away. Take-off was scheduled for 1330 hours, so that the bombers

ABOVE A USAF C–47

BELOW Crews of the 376th Bomb Group being briefed in Libya, 1943.

would arrive in the target area around dusk and make the return flight in darkness, arriving back at Soluk by midnight.

The records show that 11 of the B-24s attacked the primary target, the remainder bombing the secondary. Some suffered flak damage, and yet others had engine trouble on the way home; desert sand is not kind to aero-engines, and this was a constant problem. But by 2400 hours all the bombers except one were safely home. The missing aircraft was 'Lady Be Good'.

Then, a few minutes past midnight, the control tower at Benina received a call from the missing aircraft. Hatton informed the controller that he was unable to locate his home airfield because of dense cloud that covered the whole North African coast, and that he was growing concerned about his dwindling fuel reserves. He requested a radio fix so that he could home in on Benina.

Benina tower gave the fix as requested – but 'Lady Be Good' never arrived. A sea search the next day failed to find any trace of the bomber or its crew. They were assumed to have crashed and perished in the Mediterranean.

Only when the air force investigators pieced together the story of the last flight of 'Lady Be Good' 16½ years later did the truth come to light – and it revealed a tragic chain of circumstances. When Lieutenant Hatton called for the radio fix, the Liberator was already a long way to the southeast of Benina and heading steadily into the wastes of the Libyan Desert.

ABOVE The loneliest crew position of all – rear gun turret of a Liberator.

LEFT Fine air-to-air shot of Liberators en route to the target.

OPPOSITE PAGE, BOTTOM The 'Lady be Good' as it was discovered by the search team.

The first factor in the tragedy was a change in the weather. Unknown to the crew, the wind had veered to the northeast and increased in speed. An aircraft's speed over the ground depends on the direction and velocity of the winds it encounters, so that with an unexpectedly strong tailwind 'Lady Be Good' made much faster progress southwards than its captain realized.

The second factor was the radio fix itself. Direction-finding equipment was fairly primitive in 1943, relying on the turning of a loop aerial. When the aerial was so aligned that it picked up the radio signal at maximum strength from the aircraft, the latter's bearing was shown in degrees on a direction indicator. This was duly registered by the Benina controller, who informed Hatton that the Liberator was on a true bearing of 330° from Benina – in other words, somewhere on a line extending northwestwards from the airfield. Armed with this information, all the bomber's navigator had to do then was to compensate for magnetic variation, wind speed and velocity in order to bring the bomber overhead, where it could be talked down through the cloud for a safe landing.

But there was a serious flaw. The actual bearing of the Liberator was 150° from Benina – in other words, to the southeast. This was the exact reciprocal of 330° on the compass face. With the equipment at their disposal, the control tower staff at Benina had no means of knowing what had happened. They still believed that the B-24 was heading in from the Mediterranean. They had no reason to think otherwise, and the direction-finding signal sounded exactly the same from 150° as it would have done from 330°.

ABOVE The fuselage interior of the wrecked aircraft. The coffee found in the flasks was still drinkable.

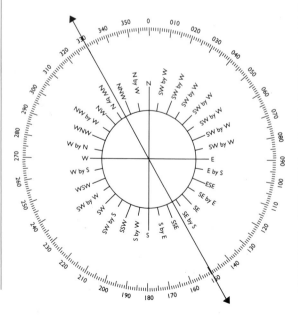

LEFT The equipment of the 'Lady be Good' registered the exact reciprocal of the aircraft's true bearing.

So 'Lady Be Good' and its crew flew steadily on into the desert, and to disaster. What must have passed through the minds of the unfortunate crew in those desperate, lost hours that followed, we can only guess at. But at some point, with his fuel practically exhausted, Lieutenant Hatton must have decided that there was only one course of action. With no chance of landing safely in the desert darkness, he ordered them to bale out.

Years later, following the initial discovery of the wreck of 'Lady Be Good', the USAF mounted a land search of the area to try to find out what had become of the crew. Eventually, a search party found the first clue in a shallow depression about eight miles northwest of the crash site; three flying boots, arranged in the shape of an arrow.

The searchers followed the direction it indicated and found more discarded items of clothing, all showing the route the airmen had been following. They must have hoped against hope that rescue would come soon, that their aircraft would be

Crash site of the 'Lady Be Good'

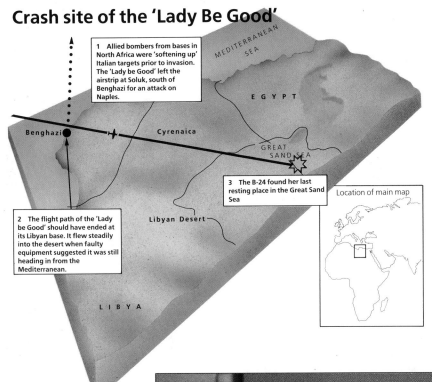

1   Allied bombers from bases in North Africa were 'softening up' Italian targets prior to invasion. The 'Lady be Good' left the airstrip at Soluk, south of Benghazi for an attack on Naples.

2   The flight path of the 'Lady be Good' should have ended at its Libyan base. It flew steadily into the desert when faulty equipment suggested it was still heading in from the Mediterranean.

3   The B-24 found her last resting place in the Great Sand Sea

Location of main map

quickly located. Perhaps they were spurred on by the belief that the Mediterranean coast was only a few miles away, a belief encouraged by that last, fatal radio fix.

It is not known if all the crew survived. Some distance further on the searchers found an empty .45 ammunition clip, as though someone had been firing his pistol in a last attempt to locate other crew members.

The searchers followed the grim trail, marked now by strips of parachute cloth which the crew must have used to shield themselves from the terrible desert sun by day and the intense cold of the nights. At last, on the edge of that fearful expanse of burning wasteland called the Great Sand Sea, the trail came to an end. Somewhere out there the crew of 'Lady Be Good' suffered their final agonies; and the sand, its contours shifting and changing constantly on the eddies of the desert wind, covered their last resting place.

RIGHT
Liberators leaving enemy territory – all too many did not make it home.

The Sub That Sank Itself

The USS *Tang* was foremost in a class of big ocean-going submarines which, during the crucial period of the Pacific War – as the American carrier task forces embarked on the long, embattled haul across the ocean towards the Japanese home islands – had wrought havoc with Japan's shipping.

The Formosa Strait was a favourite hunting ground, and it was there, at sunrise on 25 October, 1944, that the *Tang* found herself. It was her fifth war patrol in eight months of operations, and her skipper, Commander Richard H. O'Kane, had good reason to be pleased with himself.

Two nights previously, in a surface attack on a Japanese convoy, he had destroyed three tankers and two transports. Then, during the late evening of 24 October, he had made radar contact with another convoy and shadowed it through the night, making another surface attack on it at sunrise. His torpedoes hit and crippled one of the escorting warships, then another salvo struck the 7,024 ton merchantman *Matsumoto Maru*, which exploded and began to sink stern first. That brought the total number of ships sunk by the *Tang* in her eight-month career to 24, grossing 93,184 tons. No other submarine in the United States Navy could boast of such an achievement – nor, for that matter, could any other type of American warship.

The action had left the *Tang* with only one torpedo. O'Kane's Executive Officer, Lieutenant Bill Leibold, suggested jokingly that perhaps they ought to keep it as a souvenir, but O'Kane had already decided that he was going to use it against the escort vessel he had crippled in the earlier attack. He brought the submarine on to a new bearing, settled down behind the torpedo-sight on

Then came the shock. The incoming torpedo was not running on a straight track. It appeared to be moving around the *Tang* in a big circle – but the circle was getting gradually smaller in diameter. The submarine was trapped.

The men in the various compartments were unaware of the unfolding drama. The first they knew of it was when the submarine shook to a terrific explosion, somewhere near the stern. The immediate reaction of those who survived the impact was that the *Tang* must have struck a mine. The men in the three stern compartments never stood a chance. Mercifully, many of them would have been knocked unconscious by the concussion before the water poured in to inundate them.

Up above, O'Kane just had time to shout an order to close the conning-tower hatch before the torpedo struck. Then the shock of the explosion threw him and the eight others into the sea. Some of the men were injured and unable to help themselves; no one had been wearing a life-jacket. Within seconds there were only four survivors in the water: O'Kane, Leibold, Lieutenant Larry Savadkin, the Engineer Officer, and a radar specialist named

LEFT Captain Richard O'Kane, skipper of the USS *Tang*.

OPPOSITE The view from the bridge as a US submarine makes good speed on the surface.

BELOW A Japanese destroyer, seen through the periscope, goes down after a torpedo attack.

the bridge and passed the deflection angle to the bow torpedo compartment. Then he gave the order to fire. Now, he thought, the *Tang* could slip away from these dangerous waters and return to her base at Pearl Harbor.

There were eight other men on the bridge with O'Kane. Suddenly, one of them gave a shout of alarm and pointed. Several pairs of eyes picked out the phosphorescent track of a torpedo, spearing directly towards the submarine. It was still some distance away, off the port bow. O'Kane was alerted and immediately issued orders for evasive action. The submarine increased speed and the helmsman put on full right rudder.

Busy as he was, O'Kane found time to wonder where the attack had come from. There were no Japanese warships within range apart from the one he had recently attacked, which was clearly out of action, and constant sonar sweeps had not revealed the presence of an enemy submarine. The *Tang* was fitted with the most modern detection equipment; it was quite inconceivable that she could have been taken by surprise.

And yet there was the torpedo, still coming towards her. O'Kane was confident that it would miss. He had taken the appropriate evasive action in plenty of time.

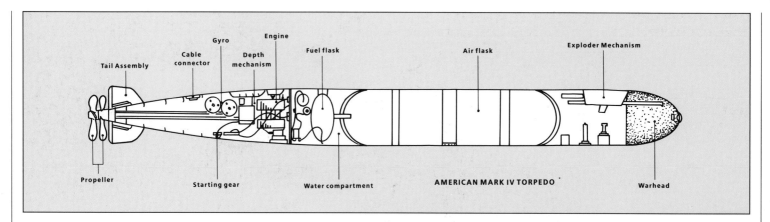

Tail Assembly · Cable connector · Gyro · Depth mechanism · Engine · Fuel flask · Air flask · Exploder Mechanism

Propeller · Starting gear · Water compartment · **AMERICAN MARK IV TORPEDO** · Warhead

Floyd Caverly. Seconds before the torpedo struck, he had come topside to report the failure of some of his equipment.

With tons of water pouring into her, the *Tang* went down stern first with terrifying speed. There was another shock as her stern struck the bottom at a depth of 180 ft. A considerable length of her bow section still protruded above the surface.

O'Kane's split-second action in ordering the closure of the conning-tower hatch had undoubtedly saved lives, but the plight of the men inside the submarine was desperate. Several were seriously injured and there was a fire in the forward battery compartment. It was quickly extinguished, but the interior of the boat continued to fill with smoke and fumes from the smouldering cables.

One of the men trapped in the boat was a seaman mechanic named Clayton Oliver who recovered his senses to find himself next to the control that governed No. 2 ballast tank. He knew that for the survivors to have a chance of using their escape apparatus – Momsen Lungs – the boat would need to be more or less on an even keel. He operated the control and, as water rushed into the ballast tank, the submarine began to settle. Afterwards, Oliver saw to the destruction of the ship's documents in the control room before making his way to the forward torpedo compartment with several other survivors.

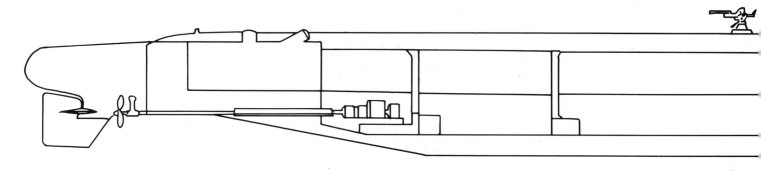

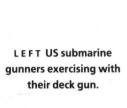

RIGHT The aft engine room of a US Fleet submarine.

TOP LEFT An American Mark IV torpedo.

LEFT US submarine gunners exercising with their deck gun.

BELOW Interior of an American submarine like the USS *Tang*. The first explosion destroyed the first 3 compartments near the stern.

Meanwhile, escorting Japanese warships had begun a random depth-charge attack in the vicinity of the convoy the *Tang* had attacked. None of the depth-charging came near enough to damage the stricken submarine, but the attack lasted for four hours – and to men already injured and sick the continual concussions were nightmarish. Some of them lapsed into unconsciousness. They had no choice but to postpone any escape attempt, because even at a distance the underwater shock waves could kill a man.

When the attack ended, the 30 survivors, under the direction of the Torpedo Officer, Lieutenant Jim Flanagan, set about preparing to abandon the submarine. Flanagan ordered four men into the escape chamber and an inflatable rubber dinghy was passed to them before the flooding-up routine was started.

Thirty minutes later, the chamber was drained and opened. Three of the men were still inside, half-drowned and barely conscious. Only one had managed to get out, and Flanagan learned later that he had not reached the surface.

Flanagan ordered a second attempt. This time, five men squeezed into the chamber. The flooding-up and draining-down process took 45 minutes, and when it was over Flanagan found that only three had made their escape. Two were still inside.

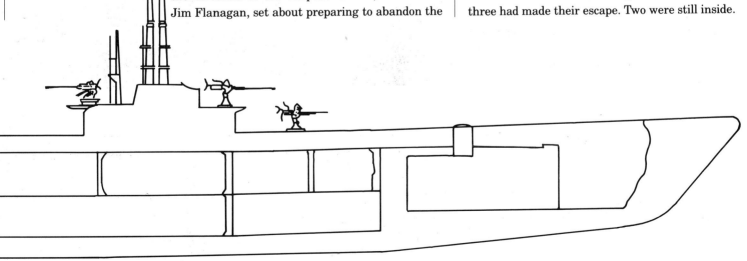

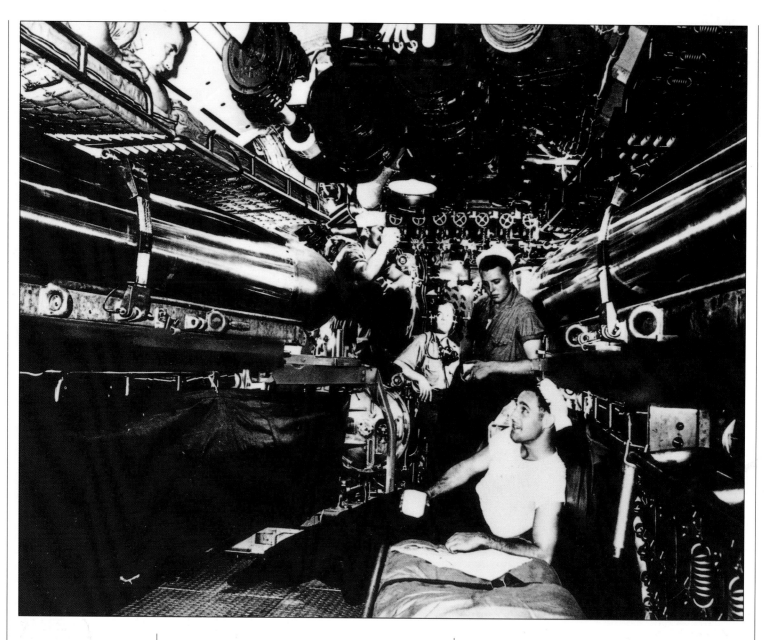

ABOVE Submariners relaxing in the forward torpedo room between actions against the enemy. On the *Tang,* there was no hope for the men trapped here.

By this time Flanagan was at the end of his strength, and the supervision of the escape operation was undertaken by another officer, Ensign Pearce. Under his direction four more men entered the chamber, but although all of them safely cleared the escape hatch only one survived the ascent to the surface.

Pearce persuaded the exhausted Flanagan to leave with the fourth group. As Flanagan pulled himself laboriously up the cable that led from the escape chamber to the surface, where it was attached to a buoy, he felt a series of concussions from below. Before his departure, he had noticed that the fire in the battery room had flared up again and was so fierce that the paint on the inside of the bulkhead separating the forward torpedo room from where the fire was raging had begun to blister. Worse still, the rubber gasket forming the seal around the watertight door had begun to smoulder in the intense heat. It must have given way. There would be no hope of escape now for those still trapped in the wreck of the *Tang.*

Of the 88 officers and ratings who had formed the crew of the *Tang,* only 15 survived to be picked up by Japanese vessels. They included O'Kane, Leibold, Flanagan and Oliver. For these men, the ordeal was just beginning. Thrown into a prison camp on Formosa, they were subjected to appalling treatment by the Japanese – some of whom were survivors from the torpedoed freighter *Matsumoto Maru,* allowed into the camp to exact their revenge on the Americans.

The Japanese made much propaganda capital out of the sinking of the USS *Tang*, which had been a thorn in their side for so long. Meanwhile, the US Naval Staff puzzled over the submarine's fate. They were not prepared to accept that she had been destroyed by the Japanese. How she had really met her end remained a complete mystery throughout the closing months of the war.

When the prison camp at Omori, where the *Tang*'s survivors were held, was liberated by American troops on 29 August, 1945, they found only nine of the original 15 still alive. Commander O'Kane and Lieutenant Flanagan were among them. O'Kane was later awarded the Congressional Medal of Honor.

It was O'Kane who provided the true story behind the sinking of the *Tang*. She had sunk herself with her last torpedo. It had left the tube all right, but something had gone wrong with its steering gear and it had come round and headed for its mother craft.

Bill Leibold had been right. They should have kept that last torpedo as a souvenir after all.

LEFT A barrier between life and death: the watertight door in a US Fleet submarine.

BELOW Crowded accommodation in a US submarine. In an emergency, every man had to know exactly what to do – instantly.

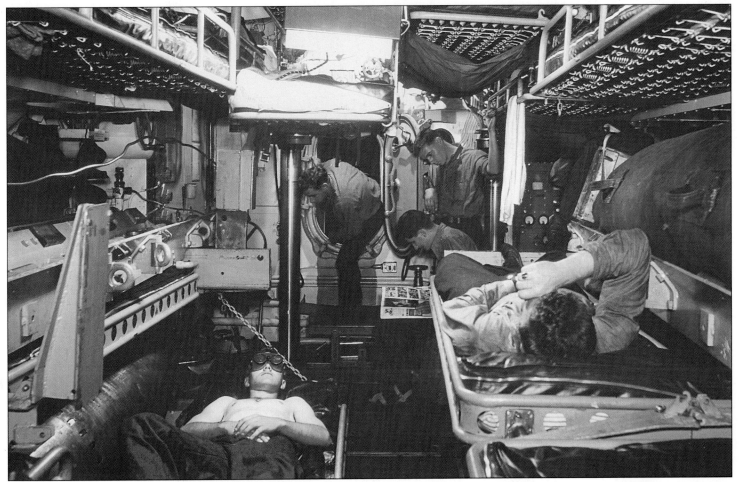

The Strange Case of Rudolf Hess

Just after 10 o'clock on the evening of 10 May, 1941, an air defence radar station on the northeast coast of England detected an unidentified aircraft approaching British airspace. As it approached the coast it dived to pick up speed, crossed the Scottish border and headed almost due west at low level. Two Defiant night fighters were scrambled from the RAF base at Prestwick to intercept the intruder, but it was travelling so fast that they failed to catch it.

The mysterious aircraft, a Messerschmitt 110, flew over the town of Kilmarnock, 25 miles south of Glasgow. When it reached the sea the pilot turned south and followed the coast for a few miles before heading back inland. He then took the aircraft up to 6,500 ft and baled out to land near the village of Eaglesham, where he was arrested. The Messerschmitt crashed nearby. It was 11.09.

Later that night, Wing Commander the Duke of Hamilton, who was in charge of sector operations at Turnhouse, near Edinburgh, was awakened with the astonishing news that the German pilot was demanding to see him. In 1936 the duke, known affectionately as 'Douglo' to his RAF colleagues, had visited the Berlin Olympics and met several *Luftwaffe* pilots. He had carefully noted their names, but had never heard of the man who was now asking to see him – a man calling himself Alfred Horn.

Mystified, Douglo went off to Maryhill Barracks, Glasgow, where the prisoner was being held. The next day he returned to Turnhouse to find that two pilots from the fighter squadron he had previously commanded, No. 602, had dropped in for a visit. They were Flight Lieutenants George Chater and Sandy Johnstone. Clearly flustered, Douglo took

them to one side.

'Don't think me mad,' he told them, 'but I think Rudolf Hess is in Glasgow!'

Rudolf Hess – no less a person than Hitler's deputy. It couldn't be true, but it was. The Duke of Hamilton's official report on his meeting with Hess reads as follows:

LEFT The wreckage of
Hess's Messerschmitt.

BELOW LEFT
Ploughman David
McLean, the man who
caught Hess, seen with
his mother – who offered
the Nazi a cup of tea.

BELOW Hess's
appearance in Scotland
made front page news.

19

RIGHT Hess delighted in sharing the rostrum with Hitler at Nazi Party rallies.

ABOVE LEFT Hess, pictured here before the war, was an accomplished pilot.

'I entered the room of the prisoner accompanied by the Interrogating Officer and the Military Officer on guard. The prisoner, who I had no recollection of ever having seen before, at once requested that I should speak to him alone. I then asked the other officers to withdraw, which they did.

'The German opened by saying that he had seen me in Berlin at the Olympic Games in 1936 and that I had lunched in his house. He said: "I do not know if you recognize me, but I am Rudolf Hess." He went on to say that he was on a mission of humanity and that the Führer did not want to defeat England and wished to stop fighting. His friend Albrecht Haushofer told him that I was an Englishman who, he thought, would understand his (Hess's) point of view. He had consequently tried to arrange a meeting with me in Lisbon. [Albrecht Haushofer, an intellectual and a close friend of Hess, had attempted to write to the Duke via Lisbon in September 1940; the letter had been intercepted by British Intelligence.]

'Hess went on to say that he had tried to fly to Dungavel [the home of the Duke of Hamilton] and this was the fourth time he had set out, the first time being in December. On the three previous occasions he had turned back owing to bad weather. He had not attempted to make this journey during the time when Britain was gaining victories in Libya, as he thought his mission might then be interpreted as weakness, but now that Germany had gained success in North Africa and Greece, he was glad to come . . .

'He then went on to say that the Führer was convinced that Germany would win the war, possibly soon, but certainly in one, two or three years. He wanted to stop the unnecessary slaughter that would otherwise inevitably take place.

'He asked me if I could get together leading members of my party to talk things over with a view to making peace proposals. I replied that there was now only one party in this country. He then said he could tell me what Hitler's peace terms would be. First, he would insist on an arrangement whereby our two countries would never go to war again.

'I questioned him as to how that arrangement could be brought about, and he replied that one of the conditions, of course, was that Britain would give up her traditional policy of always opposing the strongest power in Europe. I then told him that if we made peace now, we would be at war again certainly within two years. He asked why, to which I replied that if a peace agreement was possible, the arrangement could have been made before the war started, but since Germany chose war in preference to peace at a time when we were most anxious to preserve peace, I could put forward no hope of a peace agreement now . . . From press photographs and Albrecht Haushofer's description of Hess, I believe that the prisoner was indeed Hess himself.'

ABOVE Hess, on the right, seen with other members of the Nazi hierarchy.

BELOW A Messerschmitt 110, similar to the one in which Hess flew to Scotland.

So do the majority of historians who have investigated the Hess incident since the war, although there are those who still maintain that the man who parachuted into Scotland was an imposter, and not the real Hess at all. That theory is at variance with historical fact. If the airman had been an imposter, Hitler and the other leading members of the Nazi hierarchy must surely have known about it – but Hitler's reaction to the defection is a matter of record. His interpreter, Dr Paul Schmidt, recalled that it was 'as though a bomb had struck the Berghof'. General Keitel found the Führer pac-

ZUM FALL HESS

England vom Kontinent vertrieben

Luftwaffe bedroht britische Städte mit völliger Vernichtung

Täglich neue Erfolge der U-Boote

Grossbritanniens Verbindungen mit dem überseeischen Weltreich ernstlich bedroht

10. Mai 1941: Rudolf Hess, Stellvertreter des Führers, fliegt nach England

KÜRZLICH hat die englische Regierung ihre erste ausführliche Schilderung der Ankunft von Rudolf Hess in Grossbritannien gegeben.

Hess legte den Flug in einer Me 110 zurück und landete am Abend des 10. Mai 1941 mittels Fallschirms in Schottland. Hess, der die Uniform eines Hauptmannes der Luftwaffe trug, nannte sich Alfred Horn und verlangte, „in besonderem Auftrag" den Herzog von Hamilton zu sprechen.

Am folgenden Morgen, Sonntag den 11. Mai um zehn Uhr morgens, wurde Rudolf Hess am Orte seiner einstweiligen Internierung dem Oberstleutnant der *Royal Air Force*, Herzog von Hamilton, vorgeführt. Hess, der behauptete, den Herzog von den Olympischen Spielen her zu kennen — woran der Herzog sich allerdings nicht erinnern konnte — erklärte, sein Besuch sei seiner Sorge um das Schicksal der Menschheit entsprungen. Hitler wisse mit Bestimmtheit, er werde früher oder später siegen; Hess aber wolle unnötiges Blutvergiessen vermeiden.

Der Herzog von Hamilton erstattete Bericht über diese Unterhaltung. Darauf flog ein Beamter des Britischen

ing up and down his study mumbling that Hess had gone crazy. The shock was profound, and it was real.

The real mystery surrounding the Hess affair is three pronged. The first part involves the flight itself.

Hess was adamant that he had taken off from Augsburg, in Bavaria, and flown directly to Scotland. That could not have been true. The aircraft that crashed in Scotland was a Messerschmitt 110D, which had a normal range of 565 miles and a maximum range, with external fuel tanks, of 850 miles. The straight-line distance from Augsburg to

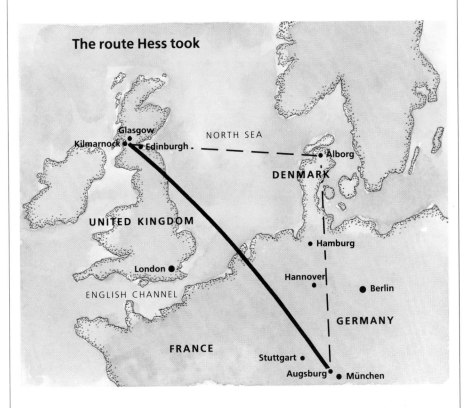

The route Hess took

Glasgow is 900 miles.

There is little doubt that Hess actually did depart from Augsburg; there were plenty of witnesses to substantiate the fact later, and after the war a photograph showing his departing aircraft came to light. But the photograph also revealed that the Messerschmitt was not fitted with long-range fuel tanks. Even if it had been, it could still not have reached Scotland.

So Hess must have landed somewhere to refuel. The most likely place is Aalborg, in Denmark, and this gives rise to the second question: was Hess actively assisted there by someone who knew what he was doing?

It is entirely possible that Hess did not act alone, and it may be significant that his friend Albrecht Haushofer was murdered in the purge that followed the 'bomb plot' attempt on Hitler's life in July, 1944. Haushofer was known to have been in contact with Admiral Canaris, the head of German military intelligence or *Abwehr*. Canaris had been tacitly opposed to Hitler's policies for some time, and although he did not actively involve himself in the bomb plot, he gave a great deal of help to the conspirators. He paid for it in a concentration camp in the spring of 1945, when he was executed.

The possibility that Canaris was in some way involved with Hess's flight to Scotland three years before the bomb plot cannot be discounted. Hitler was kept in ignorance of much that went on in the *Abwehr*; the organization was much feared in German military circles, and Canaris had the ability to open many secret doors without the knowledge of higher authority. Whether or not he did back Hess's mission was a secret he took with him to the grave.

The second aspect of this mystery concerns the man. As the world knows, Rudolf Hess was tried at Nuremberg following his captivity in Britain and sentenced to life imprisonment in Spandau Gaol. It is on record that during the years of his captivity he had the worst medical record of any war crimes prisoner. He was clearly a hypochondriac; every time a new doctor took over duty in the prison Hess tried to capture his attention with a series of pretended ailments, yet the doctors failed to find anything physically wrong with him.

One of his claims was that he suffered from bouts of amnesia, failing to recall what should have been

RIGHT Hess seen having a meal during his trial at Nuremberg.

familiar events and to recognize the faces of former friends. Such claims lent credence to the rumours that the man in Spandau was not Rudolf Hess at all, but a substitute; that the real Hess had been murdered back in 1941, when his plan to fly to Britain was discovered; and that a 'double' was permitted to fly the mission in his place. It would seem to have been a singularly pointless exercise.

In Spandau, Hess remained fanatically proud of his title of Deputy Führer. He withdrew completely, building up a protective mental wall around himself. He became terrified of anything that threatened to penetrate it; often, when he was exercising out of doors and a jet aircraft passed overhead, he would block his ears and screw his eyes tightly shut, as though refusing to believe that there was a world outside the grim walls of his prison.

The third question to be asked is whether Hess had sympathizers in Britain. The Duke of Hamilton was certainly not one of them, but the fact remains that thhere were those in high circles, either inside the British government or close to it, who would have liked to help bring about a negotiated end to the war with Germany. If this is indeed so the facts will not be released until the year 2041, for certain government files on the Hess affair remain closed until then under the very convenient hundred-year rule, which precludes the release of highly sensitive information.

And there is the tailpiece, a mystery within the mystery. On 17 August, 1987, Rudolf Hess, a sick and frail old man of 93, committed suicide by hanging himself. Yet he could barely stand, and his fingers could not tie a simple knot in a piece of string, let alone fashion a noose. One does not have to search very far to reach the conclusion that Hess was murdered, but for what motive it is not clear.

But as far as his flight to Britain is concerned, and the volumes of speculation that have emerged subsequently, perhaps it is fitting to let the then British Prime Minister, Winston S. Churchill, have the final word.

'I never', he wrote, 'attached any serious importance to this escapade.'

BELOW Churchill – seen on the left at the Yalta Conference – did not attach much importance to the Hess affair.

25

The Man Who Fought Alone

Simon Goodwin

n 9 April, 1945, with the end of the war in Europe only a month away, a group of prisoners were brutally murdered by SS guards in Dachau concentration camp and their bodies hurled into the furnaces of the crematorium. There was nothing particularly remarkable about the murderous act; in Dachau it happened almost every hour of every day.

Nor was there apparently anything remarkable about one of the victims, a 42-year-old carpenter called Georg Elser. He was an insignificant man, and yet he had been held in Dachau as a 'prominent' political prisoner. It was small wonder, for Georg Elser was involved in a plot that might have changed the course of history.

In November, 1939, within weeks of the outbreak of World War Two, Elser had come dangerously close to assassinating Adolf Hitler.

The plot was simple enough. On 8 November every year, the anniversary of the abortive 1923 Beer Hall Putsch in Munich – which started as a Nazi bid to seize power and ended with Hitler and his henchmen being arrested – the Führer made a commemorative speech to the 'old guard', the veterans of the early days of the Nazi party, in that same beer cellar. Although the Putsch had been a fiasco, in the eyes of Hitler's followers it made him a patriot and a hero, and Nazi propaganda exploited the image to the full. The anniversary speech was the perfect opportunity to blow Hitler and other leading Nazis to kingdom come.

The plan to kill him was devised by 52-year-old Karl Kuch, the leader of a three-man German Communist cell. With the full approval of his superiors in Moscow, Kuch began to lay plans for planting an explosive device in the cellar in the

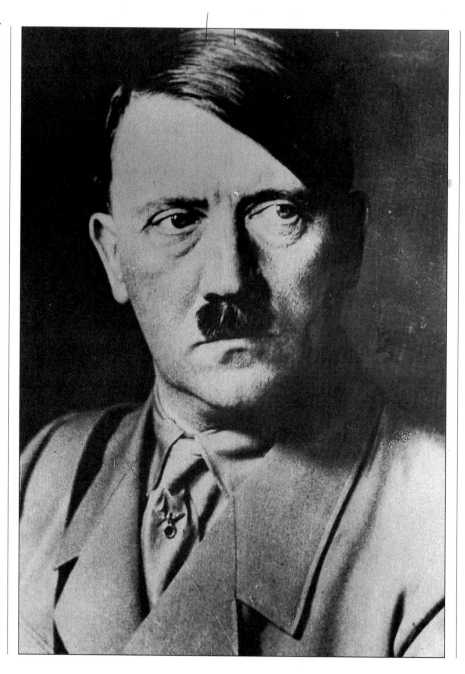

INSET Poster depicting the German invasion of Russia, 2 years after the plan to assassinate Hitler.

early months of 1939. But on 29 May – Whit Monday – Kuch received word that the Gestapo were on his trail. He decided that it was time to get out of Germany, and drove south at high speed in the direction of Switzerland.

He never made the border. His car went out of control on a dangerous stretch of road in the Swabian Alps and crashed, killing both Kuch and his wife, his only passenger.

Kuch's deputy, a waiter named Ketterer, went underground and abandoned all notions of continuing with the assassination plot. Not so the third member of the cell – Georg Elser.

Born on 4 January, 1903, Elser had a miserable childhood at the hands of a drunken and violent father. He was rescued by his uncle, who brought him up and sent him to technical school. He learned his trade as a cabinet-maker and did well at it, being an exceptionally skilled craftsman, but in 1937 he found himself unemployed for the first time in his life.

The unemployed in Germany in the 1930s presented an ideal target for Communist propaganda,

ABOVE AND OPPOSITE The two faces of Adolf Hitler – the moody introvert and the fiery, compelling orator.

INSET Poster depicting the German invasion of Russia, 2 years after the plan to assassinate Hitler.

LEFT Hitler with his propaganda minister, Josef Goebbels, who exploited beer cellar rallies to the full.

RIGHT Hitler speaking to a Hitler Youth rally in front of the Feldherrnhalle, Munich, 9 November, 1934.

and Elser began to drift along to occasional Communist meetings. In Königsbronn, he joined the group led by Karl Kuch and helped to print and distribute Communist leaflets. Kuch also gave Elser a job making wooden crates for his firm, which manufactured pianos.

When Elser learned of Kuch's death, he decided to carry on with the assassination plan alone. Meticulously, over a period of three months, he manufactured his bomb, stealing explosives from a nearby quarry. He almost came to grief in the process. In the summer of 1939 Eugen Elser, Georg's uncle, who was working in a field behind his house, heard a loud explosion and saw his nephew run out of the garden shed, surrounded by a cloud of smoke. Eugen shouted to him and asked what the matter was; Georg replied that he had just been trying out 'a little experiment'.

In between building the bomb, Elser frequently visited the beer cellar to familiarize himself with its layout and to win the confidence of the staff. Through chatting to the waitresses, he found out a piece of information that was vital to his plan: the exact spot on which Hitler stood while making his speech to the veterans. The dais was close by a huge pillar. It was about 3 ft in diameter, and made of reinforced concrete which was encased in wood panelling.

One night in August, 1939, Elser hid in a toilet adjacent to the cellar just before the place was locked up for the night. No one noticed his absence as the crowd of noisy revellers went home. Emerging from his hiding place, he cut out a section of the pillar's wooden casing with a fretsaw and fixed hinges on it, replacing it as a small door. In the cellar's dim light, it was impossible to see that it had been tampered with. He put the rubble he had dug out of the cavity into a cardboard box and disposed of it later.

From the middle of August until 6 November Elser adopted the same tactics, working in the beer cellar almost every night. He dared not use a hammer, which made his task formidably difficult. To remove the concrete, he had to bore holes in the pillar and lever out the chunks with a chisel. He had calculated that 20 lb of dynamite should be enough to bring the pillar crashing down, but he had to make the cavity big enough to conceal the whole mechanism of his bomb, which was quite a bulky affair.

LEFT The scene inside the beer cellar during Hitler's anniversary speech, shortly before Elser's assassination attempt.

Alle Kraft gespannt!
TOTALER KRIEG-
KÜRZESTER KRIEG!

ABOVE One of Hitler's favourite themes after the invasion of Poland in 1939 was to exhort the German people into an all-out war effort.

OPPOSITE And another was to secure the return of Germany's colonies, stripped from her after World War One.

By 5 November, the preparations were almost complete. The explosive had been placed in the pillar: only the mechanism had to be fitted now.

On the evening of 5 November, 1939, at about 9.30, Elser brought his clockwork mechanism into the cellar. There was a dance in progress and he went up into the gallery, where there were not many people. Towards the end of the dance, he went down into the cellar and concealed himself in a dark corner behind the pillar. There he waited until everyone had gone, the lights were out and the cellar closed.

After half an hour he went up to the pillar, opened the little door and installed the mechanism in the cavity, checking that both its clocks were accurate. By the time he had finished it was about six o'clock on the morning of 6 November. He left the cellar by the usual route, which was through an emergency exit in the kitchens.

Throughout the whole of the next day, Elser knew no peace of mind. Was the bomb mechanism still working all right? Was the ticking of the clocks loud enough to be heard? That night, he slipped back into the cellar, crept up to the pillar and listened at the improvised door. He could hear the mechanism ticking away inside. Just to be certain that all was well, he opened the door with his penknife and looked inside. Both clocks were still keeping perfect time.

At noon on 8 November, Elser boarded a train for Constance. He hoped to cross the border into Switzerland that evening. The border was only a few hundred yards from the station; it was dark, and all he had to do was climb over the wall of a school playground, run across a few gardens, and he would be in Switzerland.

It was sheer bad luck that led to his capture. As he crossed the school playground he paused by an open window. Someone had switched on a radio in the room beyond to listen to the beginning of the Führer's speech. Elser paused to listen too – and was suddenly caught in a German border guard's torch beam. He was arrested and taken to a nearby observation post. The guards inside were not interested in him for the time being; they too were intent on Hitler's words.

Elser also listened, quite calmly at first. Then, at 8.55, he suddenly became agitated. The speech was drawing to a close, much earlier than in previous years. Normally, Hitler would have gone on for another 30 minutes at least. Elser had staked everything on it. The bomb was timed to explode at 9.20.

At 9.05, Adolf Hitler left the beer cellar. By that time, Georg Elser was on his way to Gestapo headquarters.

At 9.20, precisely on time, the bomb exploded. One of the waitresses, Maria Strobel, remembered the next few seconds.

'I didn't hear an explosion. I only felt a tremendous wall of air pressure hit me and I was blown clean through the swing doors, almost as far as the main entrance. When I came to, I found myself lying among a wilderness of shattered furniture, broken beer tankards and torn tapestries. I was half buried under masonry, and almost choked with a thick cloud of dust. I could hear cries. Behind me, the whole roof of the cellar had caved in.'

prominent prisoner in Dachau and was fairly well treated, being allowed to work as a carpenter and even to leave the camp for short periods.

It may be that Elser's story – that he worked completely alone – was untrue. Perhaps Hitler himself knew, or at least suspected, that Elser was a puppet, his strings being manipulated by others – perhaps even some of the Führer's close associates. Maybe Hitler believed that in the fullness of time, Elser would voluntarily reveal his secret.

But whatever unrevealed truths there might have been, they died with the carpenter in a burst of machine-gun fire on that April morning in 1945.

LEFT Did Hitler suspect that Elser was the puppet of a large anti-Nazi organization?

The collapsing ceiling had buried most of the people in the cellar beneath its debris. Seven lost their lives, 63 were injured.

The Gestapo tried frantically to bludgeon out of Elser the names of any accomplices, and they failed. Predictably, Propaganda Minister Josef Goebbels lost no time in blaming the British secret service as the real culprit.

For some time, the British and German secret services had been sparring with one another in neutral Holland. The Germans had succeeded in feeding the British a certain amount of false information, including the names of a number of German army officers who were allegedly plotting to depose Hitler. Captain Payne Best, a British intelligence officer stationed in Holland, tried to contact the ringleader of this mysterious resistance movement, and had several inconclusive meetings just across the Dutch frontier with German officers who claimed to represent it. In fact the officers were loyal, and on 9 November, 1939 the Germans succeeded in kidnapping both Best and a colleague, Major Stevens.

Best, Stevens and the driver of their car were taken to the concentration camp at Sachsenhausen, where Elser was also imprisoned for a time. There the Germans tried to make them admit that British intelligence had been behind Elser's attempt to kill Hitler, but without success. As Walter Schellenberg – the wartime head of German counter-espionage – later admitted, there was absolutely no connection between the two.

The real mystery surrounding Elser lies in the fact that he was allowed to remain alive for so long. On Hitler's personal orders he was classed as a

The *Cap Arcona* Tragedy

O n the morning of 3 May, 1945, the sky over northern Germany and the Baltic Sea was bleak, misty and overcast.

The Germans welcomed the bad visibility, because it gave some respite from the Allied fighter-bombers which, for days now, had been mercilessly pounding the shipping crammed into the north German ports or clustered offshore. The ships were packed with military per-

sonnel and equipment of all kinds, most of which was bound for Norway, where the Germans planned to make a last stand.

Most of the anti-shipping attacks were carried out by the RAF's Second Tactical Air Force, although RAF Coastal Command and the US Ninth Air Force also took part. But it was the RAF's Hawker Typhoon fighter-bombers that the Germans feared most of all. Armed with four 20 mm cannon, the Typhoon could carry up to 1,000 lb of bombs or

BOTTOM RAF Coastal
Command played a large
part in anti-shipping
strikes.

ABOVE A Hawker
Typhoon fighter bomber.
The attacks on Lübeck
Bay in 1945 were carried
out by these aircraft.

eight rocket projectiles. A full salvo of the latter
had a destructive force equal to a broadside from a
battle-cruiser, enough to rip a ship apart.

Ever since the Allied landings in Normandy in
June, 1944, the Typhoons had harried the retreat-
ing German forces across Europe, inflicting appalling casualties on them. Now they were taking part
in the last act, before the final curtain fell on
Hitler's thousand-year Reich.

On the afternoon of 3 May the weather cleared,
and the Second Tactical Air Force unleashed its
Typhoon squadrons against the enemy shipping in
Lübeck Bay, where several large vessels had been
sighted by air reconnaissance. The four squadrons
of No. 123 Wing were briefed to carry out the
mission. Nos. 184, 263 and 198 Squadrons were
armed with cannon and rockets, while No. 197
Squadron carried cannon and bombs.

It was this squadron that carried out the first
attack, on what the pilots described as a 'two-funnel
cargo liner of 10,000 tons with steam up in Lübeck
Bay'. She was in fact the 21,046-ton passenger
liner *Deutschland*, which was in the process of being
fitted out as a hospital ship. The Typhoon pilots
had no means of knowing this, because the ship
carried only one small red cross marking, painted
on one side of a funnel. At the time of the attack
the *Deutschland* carried only 80 crew members and
a small 26-strong medical team.

The ship was hit by four rockets, one of which
failed to explode. Another started a small fire
which was quickly extinguished. No one was hurt
in the attack. Afterwards, the medical team went
ashore and the captain, anxious to surrender,
ordered white sheets to be draped over the ship's
sides and the lifeboats to be made ready for a speedy
departure.

The second attack was delivered by nine Typhoons
of No. 198 Squadron. They were led by Group Captain Johnny Baldwin, who also commanded No.

123 Wing. The attack was directed against two vessels, a large three-funnel liner and a smaller ship moored nearby. It was devastatingly successful. Some 40 rockets struck the bigger vessel, the 60-lb warheads penetrating her hull to explode inside. She was soon ablaze from stem to stern. Thirty more rockets hit the smaller ship, which developed a heavy list and began to sink, belching smoke.

The third attack was made by No. 263 Squadron. Once again, the *Deutschland* was the target. As the Typhoons came in her crew scrambled into the lifeboats and made for the shore, unharmed. The *Deutschland* was set on fire and was sunk a few minutes later by the bombs of No. 197 Squadron's Typhoons.

The RAF pilots headed back to their bases along the river Elbe. But the next day, British forces occupied the port of Lübeck – and the full horror of what had happened was revealed.

The ships had been filled to capacity, not with German troops being evacuated to Norway – but with thousands of concentration camp inmates.

As the war in Europe approached its inevitable end, orders had been issued by *Reichsführer* Heinrich Himmler, head of the SS, that no concentration camp inmates were to be allowed to fall

A B O V E An RAF Typhoon flies low over enemy territory.

R I G H T Route taken by RAF Typhoons from Alhorn, near Bremen.

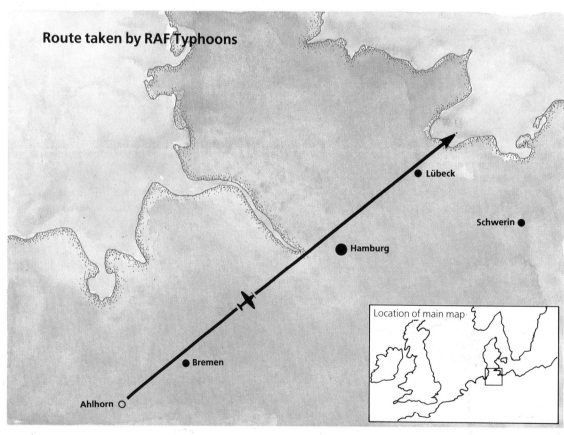

Route taken by RAF Typhoons

Lübeck

Schwerin

Hamburg

Bremen

Ahlhorn

Location of main map

into Allied hands. Those who could still march were to be moved away from the Allied line of advance; the remainder were to be killed.

At Neuengamme, near Hamburg, where half the prisoners were either Russians or Poles, 1,000 were murdered immediately. Many of the 20,000 others were quickly dispersed, but several thousand more were herded into Lübeck during the last days of April. Some 2,300 were herded aboard a 1,936-ton freighter, the *Athen*, whose captain was threatened with death by the SS guards if he did not cooperate, and were then ferried to a three-funnel liner.

She was the 27,561-ton *Cap Arcona*. Before the war she had been known as the *Queen of the South Atlantic*, carrying out luxury cruises between Hamburg and Rio de Janeiro. Her captain, Heinrich Bertram, defied the SS for a whole day. In the end an SS officer arrived bearing an order for his execution if he did not comply. Bertram was left with no alternative, and over the next four days about 7,000 prisoners from Neuengamme were packed like sardines into the liner – a vessel with accommodation and sanitary arrangements for only 700 people in her wartime role as a troopship. In addition to the prisoners, 500 SS guards also went aboard.

Meanwhile, 3,000 more prisoners had been loaded on to another vessel, the 2,815-ton freighter *Thielbeck*. On both vessels, the prisoners were battened down for days in darkness and stinking squalor, half dead already from starvation. In addition, two large barges were filled with several hundred men, women and children from the camp at Stutthof.

On 2 May, a transfer of prisoners took place between the *Cap Arcona*, the *Thielbeck* and the *Athen*. On the following morning, 4,150 remained on the liner and 2,750 on the *Thielbeck*. Another 2,000 were on the *Athen*, whose captain decided to return to port. The SS guards protested, but according to some accounts were overwhelmed by the ship's crew.

The vessel put into Neustadt. One of the survivors, Mikelis Mezmalietis, recalled what happened next.

BELOW Heinrich Himmler, head of the SS.

'On the morning of 3 May there was a terrible explosion. After a short time one of the stronger prisoners who had been aloft ran down to tell us that the Americans [sic] had bombed the *Cap Arcona* and sunk it. Everyone who could move got very excited and tried to get to the one exit. In a moment we felt the ship starting to move fast, and then it stopped.

'Nobody spoke for an hour. Then all those who could, got up and ran out, especially the German crew; we had arrived at Neustadt. I was unable to move, and was left for dead. After perhaps another hour I crawled on all fours up to the top deck . . .

'That afternoon two strong young prisoners boarded the ship to see what they could take. They were not from my ship; they turned out to be French students. They were very surprised to see me; they went searching for other prisoners but found none. Then they carried me from the ship and took me to the barracks at Neustadt, where they washed me and put me to bed in a spare bed in their room.'

The other prisoners who got away from the *Athen* eventually made contact with advance patrols of the British Army. They were the lucky ones.

On board the stricken, blazing *Cap Arcona*, more than 4,000 prisoners were burning to death or suffocating in the smoke. A few managed to break out and jump into the sea, where they were picked up by trawlers. More – about 350 in all, many suffering from burns – managed to escape before the liner capsized and swam ashore, only to be shot and clubbed to death by SS troops and fanatical Hitler Youth members.

Of the 2,750 prisoners on the *Thielbeck*, only about 50 managed to struggle ashore. Most of them met the same fate as the survivors of the *Cap Arcona*. There is no record of how the hundreds of prisoners in the two barges met their fate. When the British arrived, they found the barges stranded on the shore. The beaches were littered with dead. The adults had been shot, the children clubbed to death with rifle butts.

One of the first senior British officers on the scene was Brigadier Mills-Roberts, commanding No. 1 Commando Brigade. While he was at the scene of the slaughter, Field Marshal Erhard Milch – the former *Luftwaffe* general who had been sacked from his post and later made responsible for the deportation of forced labourers – came to surrender to him. Milch gave a Nazi salute, his field marshal's baton in his oustretched hand. The British brigadier snatched it from him and broke it over his head.

The man responsible for the massacre, Max Pauly – the commandant of Neuengamme concentration camp – was later tried as a war criminal in Hamburg and hanged, together with several of his

LEFT Field Marshal Erhard Milch. A British commando officer struck him over the head with his own baton.

subordinates. That should have been the end of the *Cap Arcona* affair – but it was not.

Nearly 40 years after the event, a series of sensational articles in the West German press claimed that the true facts behind the sinking of the *Cap Arcona* and the *Thielbeck* had been shrouded in mystery and secrecy for four decades. One of the claims was that British intelligence had known that the vessels were packed with concentration camp inmates and had done nothing about it. Another was that the RAF, knowing who the ships

BELOW A salvo of rockets was equivalent to a broadside from a 6-inch gun cruiser.

carried, had deliberately allowed them to be attacked in order to give pilots fresh out from England some operational experience before the war ended.

Such claims are nonsense. In fact, the British had issued clear warnings that *all* shipping in the Baltic would be subject to air attack, unless vessels displayed prominent red cross markings. None of the vessels involved carried such markings, and the RAF had no reason to believe that they were carrying anything other than troops – and perhaps members of the Nazi leadership – to sanctuary in Norway. In fact, it is not impossible that the ships were used as a convenient dumping ground for the prisoners in the hope that they *would* be sunk by Allied air attacks, completing the Nazis' dirty work for them.

Whatever the truth, one mystery surrounding the incident still remains. Mikelis Mezmalietis, the survivor from the *Athen*, told how the decks of the ship were crammed with tons of stores – sugar, rice, flour and macaroni. The *Athen* was to have remained in company with the other two ships. So who were the supplies intended for? The quantities were far greater than would have been required to meet the needs of the ships' crews and the SS guards.

It is just possible that they were intended to keep the prisoners alive while the SS used them to bargain with the Allies in order to save themselves – tragic pawns in a last, desperate gamble by murderers who had nothing to lose but their lives.

LEFT Hitler and Himmler, who consigned millions to their deaths.

The Mystery of the Murdered Redhead

In the European war, there were two centres of neutrality where the diplomats of the warring powers came into frequent contact with one another. One was Lisbon, Portugal; the other was Stockholm.

Daily contact was necessary with Sweden, which was trading with both sides. There were many personal negotiations and much secret mail, and Stockholm was continuously buzzing with espionage. The capital was also a transit point for mail *en route* to prisoner-of-war camps. Aircrews often came down in Sweden, or managed to get there after evading capture in Germany.

Many Norwegian airmen and other military personnel used Sweden as an alternative route to reach England, rather than risking the dangers of a North Sea passage in small boats. In March, 1942, President Roosevelt lent his active support to the Royal Norwegian Air Force centre in London, enabling the Norwegians to obtain two Lockheed Lodestar airliners to transport 50 of their countrymen a week from Sweden to Scotland. Some of them had been waiting 18 months for the chance to fight for the Allies.

Furthermore, Britain was obtaining special engineering products from Sweden, such as ball-bearings, machine-tool steel, fine springs and electrical resistors. The Germans were rival customers, and after the USAF raid on Schweinfurt in 1943, two British government officials were flown to Sweden in two de Havilland Mosquitos, specially modified to take one passenger each in the bomb bay. Their task was to negotiate for the purchase of Sweden's entire output of essential ball-bearings, primarily to prevent the Germans from getting hold of them, and in this they were successful.

OPPOSITE Jane Horney, Stockholm's queen of intrigue.

LEFT Roosevelt authorized Lockheed Lodestar airliners to run a shuttle service between Norway and the UK.

BELOW LEFT President Roosevelt in characteristic pose with cigarette holder.

BELOW Sweden was a refuge for aircraft damaged over Germany and unable to make it home to England.

In that year, Stockholm – the only city in northern Europe where the lights still blazed – was a hotbed of intrigue. With the war entering a crucial phase, plots and counter-plots were hatched in secrecy in the city's most exclusive night-clubs and restaurants.

Into this glittering and treacherous scene, sometime in the early months of 1943, came a beautiful redhead called Jane Horney. She swept like a whirlwind through the night-life of Stockholm. Her reign as uncrowned queen of Swedish society lasted only two years, but in that time she broke the hearts of diplomats from half the world.

And when she was murdered, she left behind her a mystery that still remains unsolved today.

Jane Horney was a Swedish citizen, although some said that she had been born in England. The truth was that no one knew her true origins. All people knew about her was that, in a matter of weeks, she became one of the leading lights of Stockholm's party life – and her escorts were almost always senior diplomats or known secret service men from half a dozen countries.

Whatever game she was playing, it was a dangerous one. Before long, the British had become convinced that Jane Horney was a German agent.

ABOVE British Government officials were secretly flown to Sweden in de Havilland Mosquitoes.

RIGHT In 1943, Stockholm was the only city in Northern Europe where the lights still blazed.

OPPOSITE ABOVE Jane pictured with her husband, Herje Cranberg.

OPPOSITE BELOW Why did Jane travel to Denmark by the shuttle service set up by the Danish resistance movement?

So had the Danes, many of whom had taken refuge in Sweden when their country was overrun in 1940. Rumours began to circulate that she had helped the Germans to track down and arrest certain key figures in the Danish resistance movement.

What neither the British nor the Danes knew, however, was that the Germans thought that she was a British agent – or at least that she was a double agent.

As 1943 wore on, Jane's activities grew even more complicated. In the summer, she acquired a new boyfriend, 54-year-old Horst Gilbert, a German who lived in Denmark and who ran the Scandinavian Telegraph Bureau. He was a major in the *Abwehr*, the German military intelligence service. He was a high official in Department Six, in charge of Scandinavian counter-espionage activities.

In the autumn of 1943, Jane travelled to Denmark frequently to see Gilbert. The strange thing was that she travelled not by the normal lines of communication, but by a secret shuttle service set up by the Danish resistance to run guns and refugees across the Kattegat and Skagerrak.

Then came a fresh intrigue: Jane became friendly with several senior officials in the hated Gestapo.

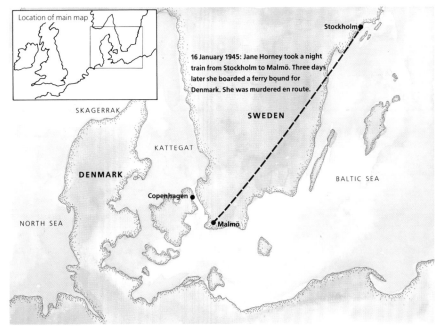

16 January 1945: Jane Horney took a night train from Stockholm to Malmö. Three days later she boarded a ferry bound for Denmark. She was murdered en route.

Location of main map

SKAGERRAK

KATTEGAT

DENMARK

SWEDEN

BALTIC SEA

Copenhagen

NORTH SEA

Malmö

Stockholm

ABOVE Jane had free passage through Sweden's ports on her frequent trips to Germany.

BELOW The British Embassy, Stockholm.

They included an agent named Hoffman, who organized the anti-resistance operations. Her expanding circle of friends also included SS *Obersturmbannführer* Seibold, the head of Department Six.

Early in 1944, equipped with a special pass that allowed her to cross the frontiers of the occupied countries without hindrance, she went to Germany several times – and on her return to Sweden, complicating her story even further, she passed information about the German intelligence system in Scandinavia to the Swedish authorities.

In March, 1944, Jane's latest boyfriend was a British intelligence officer, a major attached to the British embassy in Stockholm. No one knows whether he was sent to Stockholm with specific orders to become friendly with her, but he certainly did so. She fell head over heels in love with him. For several months they were inseparable, and then the major suddenly broke off the affair. It may be that he had learned everything there was to know about her, and was ordered to terminate the assignment. In any event, she was heartbroken and disappeared from the Stockholm scene for some weeks.

When she returned, she seemed to pay more attention to the Germans than ever before – whether because of her unhappy affair with the British officer will never be known.

The Danish resistance became very suspicious of her and their agents shadowed her everywhere, photographing her and the people she met. That autumn, the Swedish secret service, acting on information supplied by the Danes, arrested her and took her in for interrogation.

On 13 October, 1944, after three weeks, she was set free. The Swedes informed the Danes that she had been completely cleared of all suspicion, and the Danes outwardly expressed their satisfaction. Secretly, however, their top agents remained con-

ABOVE Jane had free passage through Sweden's ports on her frequent trips to Germany.

BELOW The British Embassy, Stockholm.

vinced that Jane Horney was a dangerous spy in the pay of the Nazis – and early in January, 1945 a seven-man execution squad arrived in Sweden by various routes. For the lovely redhead who had captivated Stockholm society for so long, the sands were fast running out.

On 16 January, two of the Danish agents accompanied Jane to Stockholm's Central Station. How they met her, or persuaded her to travel with them, no one can tell. They took a night train to Malmö, where rooms had been booked at the Grand Hotel.

Hotel staff later told police that *two* striking, red-haired girls were staying at the hotel, and that they were in adjoining rooms. One of them was later seen at Malmö station, boarding the Stockholm train. As part of an elaborate cover-up, it seems that the strange redhead must have changed clothes with Jane and assumed her identity for a time – long enough, at least, to allow the Danes to spirit the real Jane out of Sweden.

On the night of 19 January, Jane and her Danish companions boarded a ferry bound for Denmark. Halfway across, however, the ferry hove-to and Jane – together with two or three men – transferred to a Danish fishing boat. Several members of the ferry's crew saw this happen, but took no particular notice; such secret exchanges were routine. It was not until they were later interrogated by police that they realized something sinister had been happening.

Somewhere out there in the darkness, after the ferry had continued on its way, Jane Horney was cold-bloodedly murdered and her body thrown into the freezing water. One of the Danish agents, picked up by police in Sweden, actually confessed to the crime – and although he later withdrew the con-

fession, leaving the Swedes with no alternative but to release him through lack of evidence, there is no doubt that the murder took place.

But Jane Horney's disappearance was only the start of the mystery. As soon as the war was over, the Swedish secret service suddenly closed the file on her, as did the Danes. The British claimed that they had never heard of her, and former German *Abwehr* officers who had known her remained stubbornly silent.

The continued silence might mean that Jane Horney really was a top-ranking agent, or even a double agent. Or there might be a more intriguing and tragic explanation – that Jane was simply an adventuress, a girl about town who lived life to the full at the expense of all the secret service men who tried to use her, and who outwitted them. And who was killed because she was an embarrassment.

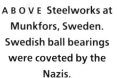

ABOVE Steelworks at Munkfors, Sweden. Swedish ball bearings were coveted by the Nazis.

LEFT Nazi spies tried hard to infiltrate Sweden's Bofors arms factories.

Hidden Treasures of World War Two

onquering armies are no respecters of property, and when the Nazis overran most of Europe in 1940 they were no exception. With many of the great cultural centres of Europe in their grasp, the Nazi leaders embarked on a systematic looting campaign of a magnitude unmatched since barbarian tribes swarmed into the Roman Empire.

Luftwaffe commander-in-chief Hermann Göring, for example, filled his fabulous estate at Karinhall with booty – paintings, sculptures and tapestries – from the occupied territories. With the Russian army on his doorstep early in 1945, he loaded the lot on to a motor convoy and headed south for the comparative sanctuary of Bavaria, where the booty was eventually recovered by American forces.

Most of the other Nazi loot was similarly recovered and returned to its rightful owners, but rumours persist to this day that a vast hoard of treasure, mainly gold bullion, still lies hidden under the waters of one or more lakes in Austria. The story goes that it was deposited there by SS *Stürmbannfuhrer* Otto Skorzeny, who led Germany's commando forces during the war.

A daring commander, it was Skorzeny who led a commando force to rescue the Italian dictator Benito Mussolini in September, 1943, after he had been overthrown and imprisoned in the wake of the Allied invasion of Italy. Mussolini was held captive in a hotel on top of the Gran Sasso d'Italia, the highest mountain range in the Abruzzi Apennines. Skorzeny and his men made a glider assault on the place, overpowered Mussolini's guards, and flew the dictator out to safety in a Storch light aircraft. Skorzeny also commanded the German special forces units. This unit operated

LEFT Mussolini was flown to safety in a Storch light aircraft.

OPPOSITE German Luftwaffe leader Hermann Göring filled his Karinhall mansion with looted art treasures.

CENTRE Stürmbannfuhrer Otto 'Scarface' Skorzeny.

BELOW Skorzeny's paratroops rescued Mussolini from captivity.

behind the Allied lines disguised as American troops during the Ardennes offensive in the winter of 1944–45.

There is little doubt that Skorzeny did succeed in amassing a sizeable personal fortune during the war, and some years later there were several well-publicized accounts by men who had served under his command and who alleged that they had been present when the bullion was hidden. Since then there have been many attempts to locate it, but all have failed.

Perhaps there is a simple explanation for the failure. Skorzeny himself was captured by American forces at the end of the war, and in 1947 he was brought before an American war crimes tribunal at Dachau. He was acquitted, and after spending some years in Fascist Spain he moved to South America, where he soon established a prosperous cement business. Perhaps he used his years in

Spain to good advantage, making clandestine visits to Austria to recover his booty before anyone else got to it and subsequently using it as capital for his business ventures.

One massive haul of Nazi treasure was discovered at the end of the war by American forces in a disused mine shaft at Quedlinburg, a few miles south of Magdeburg. The hoard consisted of medieval works of art, including gold and silver crucifixes, rock crystal flasks, a silver reliquary inlaid with precious stones and enamels, a liturgical ivory comb, various priceless gifts belonging to the warlords who ruled the old states of Germany in the ninth and tenth centuries, and – perhaps the most priceless of all – a beautifully illustrated ninth-century version of the four gospels in a gold and silver binding encrusted with gold and jewels.

The Quedlinburg treasures were removed from their hiding place by a US army lieutenant named

ABOVE Lake Como, where Mussolini's treasure is reputed to lie.

Joe T. Meador. He had taken part in the Normandy invasion of June, 1944 and had fought his way across France with an artillery unit that eventually occupied Quedlinburg. He was assigned to one of three teams searching for weapons, radio transmitters and other equipment that might be put to use by Nazi resistance fighters.

The treasure was discovered quite by accident when a drunken soldier stumbled into the mine shaft. Meador's unit was given the important task of guarding it until it could be properly catalogued and identified.

But Meador, a very knowledgeable man in matters of art, had other ideas. He quietly removed the treasure piece by piece and smuggled the items home by the very simple expedient of mailing them.

The US army, baffled by the loss of the treasure, launched an inquiry, but this ended in 1949 when

ABOVE, LEFT AND BELOW At the war's end, Allied troops found loot in mine shafts and mansions all over Germany.

47

WOMAN INVESTIGATES REAL-LIFE MYSTERY THAT RIVALS PLOT OF ANY THRILLER

Missing Nazi loot worth $$millions leads to string of grisly murders in fear-haunted village

MISSING Nazi loot worth millions has led to a string of grisly murders in a terrified Italian town in a long-lasting campaign of terror that rivals the plot of any thriller.

Nineteen people have met violent deaths over the last 11 years in the small village of Bargagli — 10 ...

'HITLER' SILVER LEFT ON SHELF FOR 30 YEARS

By TONY ALLEN-MILLS

A SET of silver cutlery which may have been part of a personal collection of Adolf Hitler's personal belongings, has surfaced at the home of an antiques dealer in Hawkhurst, Kent.

Mr David Corcoran has had the silver, monogrammed with the initials A.H., for 30 years. He said yesterday he used to joke to friends that it might have belonged to Hitler.

Looted painting dropped from Sotheby's art sale

By ROBIN SIMON, Arts Correspondent

SOTHEBY'S has withdrawn a medieval Italian painting from auction after discovering that it was stolen by Nazi troops in the war.

The painting, expected to fetch £30,000, was listed in the catalogue for yesterday's sale when Interpol in Rome raised the alarm.

The picture, of St John the Baptist, by the 15th century painter known as the Master of the Osservanza, is likely to remain in Sotheby's security vault until a row over its ownership is solved.

Mr Joe Och, a director of Sotheby's, said that the present owner, a Viennese art dealer, appears to have a legitimate title.

LEFT Looted art treasures continue to surface even now.

OPPOSITE, ABOVE General Yamashita, the 'Tiger of Malaya'.

BELOW The Malay Peninsula, occupied by General Tomozuki Yamashita's soldiers since the beginning of the war.

works, unconnected with the Quedlinburg treasure and apparently looted from France and other parts of Germany.

So, after many years, one mystery surrounding part of World War Two's lost treasures is being solved. It is an ongoing saga, because efforts are still being made to trace the missing third part of the Quedlinburg treasure.

On the other side of the world, at least one Japanese general is thought to have amassed a huge treasure hoard. He was General Tomozuki Yamashita, whose soldiers ruled the Philippines with great brutality for three long years before the islands were reoccupied by American forces.

Yamashita's name became linked with plunder and torture, and yet, unlike many other high-ranking Japanese officers, the general – who was known as the 'Tiger of Malaya' because of the lightning speed with which his forces had occupied the Malayan Peninsula at the outset of the war – allowed himself to be captured alive by the Allies.

Yamashita was tried as a war criminal and hanged in February, 1946. And with him, he took

Quedlinburg became part of East Germany. Meanwhile, Meador, having returned to civilian life, ran a hardware store in the little farm town of Whitewright, Texas, continued with his love of art, and grew orchids.

He died in 1980 at the age of 64, and soon afterwards rumours began to circulate among dealers in medieval art in New York, London, Munich and Zurich that 'something remarkable' would soon appear on the market. Then, in April, 1990, a private West German organization called the Cultural Foundation of the States announced that it had recovered one of the missing artworks – the four gospels – after paying a 'finder's fee' of $3 million to a lawyer acting for the estate of a former American soldier, a Texan. The deal had been secretly set up in Switzerland by a Bavarian art dealer, who had in his possession another item from the treasure hoard – a 1513 manuscript valued at $500,000.

Further investigations revealed that the town of Whitewright was the hiding place of all the treasures. They were widely dispersed; some were found in the offices of Meador's hardware store, some were in private homes, and still others were in safe-deposit boxes. In all, two-thirds of the treasure was recovered; all of the items were in perfect condition. In addition, German and American lawyers uncovered a new cache of art-

THAILAND

• Butterworth

• Kuala Trengganu

MALAYSIA

Location of main map

STRAIT OF MALACCA

• Kuala Lumpur

• Malacca

• Johor Bharu

SUMATRA

SINGAPORE

to the grave the secret that has baffled adventurers and fortune-hunters ever since: the whereabouts of what is rumoured to be the world's biggest hoard of treasure. He made capital out of the chaos of war by looting enormous riches, including gold and silver bars and precious stones, from temples all over Southeast Asia.

Before he surrendered himself to the Allies in 1945, Yamashita is thought to have hidden his treasure on the island of Lubang, in the Philippine group. Since the end of the war, dozens of former Japanese soldiers have searched for it, and so have official Philippine investigation teams. In 1972, the then president, Ferdinand Marcos, ordered the formation of a special army commando to search for the treasure on Lubang and elsewhere in the islands – but the soldiers drew a complete blank, as did everyone else.

Then, in 1974, new light was shed on the affair with the sudden emergence from the Lubang jungle of the man who had been called the last of the Japanese emperor's warriors – Lieutenant Hiru Onada, who carried on fighting for 29 years in the belief that the war was still in progress, and killed 39 people in the course of skirmishes with Philippine police patrols, and on forays into the island's villages in search of food.

Although Onada never admitted it, there are strong indications that he may have been the last survivor of an élite body of Japanese army troops, sent into the Philippines by Yamashita in the closing stages of the war for the sole purpose of guarding the treasure.

In 1944, he underwent a course of training in the Nakano Gekko, the Japanese military intelligence school – a routine procedure for all Japanese officers about to undertake some kind of special mission. And, almost without exception, every officer who passed through the school – and who was not killed in the fighting – committed suicide when the Japanese empire went down in defeat.

The exception was Onada, who may have been specifically ordered to carry out his mission even if the Japanese army ceased to exist. Some Philippine officials believe that the lieutenant finally gave himself up not because despair was beginning to set in, but because he was afraid that he might one day inadvertently lead a government patrol to the treasure's hiding place.

After Onada's surrender, President Marcos implemented strict controls on the movement of any tourists wishing to visit Lubang. Marcos has gone, but the controls are still in place. If the treasure really is there, the Philippine government is determined to find it first.

BELOW Was Onado ordered by Yamashita to defend the treasure even after the defeat of the Japanese Army?

BOTTOM The ultimate Japanese objective in the Pacific was Australia.

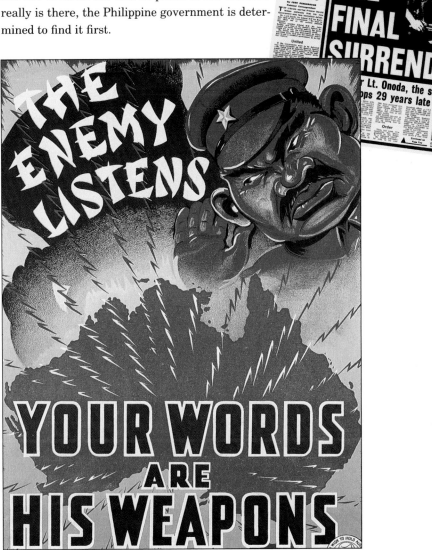

The Mystery of Germany's A-bomb

n the closing months of 1945, following the destruction of Hiroshima and Nagasaki, sensational accounts appeared in several newspapers around the world claiming that the weapons used had been developed not in the United States, but in Germany. It was also claimed that a factory for the production of uranium bombs had been set up, under the control of the SS, on the Danish island of Bornholm as the war in Europe drew to a close.

To this day, rumours persist that Germany was on the verge of producing an operational atomic bomb when the war ended. The facts, however, are rather less dramatic.

Most of the rumours had their origin in Germany itself, beginning with Hitler's wild claim that the Nazis were about to field a super-weapon that would win the war for them at one stroke. Then, in the closing days of the war, Nazi party officials went from house to house in Munich, spreading the word that an atomic bomb was about to be used.

The fact is that a team of German scientists, under the direction of the eminent physicist Professor Otto Hahn, had been actively engaged in nuclear research since 1937, and were well ahead of anyone else in theoretical work. Ironically, they published their findings as scientific papers – documents that were avidly studied by scientists in Britain and the United States. If war had broken out in 1938, the papers would never have been published. Their secrets would have remained the exclusive property of the Germans, and although the Allies would undoubtedly have pressed on with their own atomic research, it is open to doubt whether they would have produced an atomic bomb as early as they did.

By 1939, Otto Hahn knew that his discoveries, if applied practically, could lead to fission – the splitting of the uranium atom. It was some days before he realized the terrible consequences this might have. Years later, when in Allied captivity he heard for the first time that his discovery had been put to practical use in the bomb that destroyed Hiroshima, he confided to colleagues that back in 1939 he had been unable to sleep for many days and had even contemplated taking his own life.

Senior officials at the German war office were aware of the military possibilities of nuclear power several months before the outbreak of war. A ban was placed on the export of uranium compounds from Germany. But although research continued into the military application of nuclear fission, it remained a low-key, decentralized business.

Uranium was in short supply. One of the principal sources of the element was the Belgian Congo, so it came as a real windfall for the Germans when, after their armies overran the Low Countries in the summer of 1940, they captured considerable stocks of uranium held in Belgium. Before that, in April, they had invaded Norway, giving them access to the Norwegian Hydro-Electric Company's hydrogen electrolysis plant at Vemork. This was an important step forward, because the factory produced Europe's only supply of deuterium oxide, also known as heavy water. The Germans planned

to use this as a 'moderator' in their experimental atomic reactor. Heavy water is one of the substances that slows down neutrons, which are used to bombard the uranium atoms in the fission process; another is graphite, which was later used by the Allies.

The Germans would have used graphite too had it not been for the faulty calculations of a professor at Heidelberg University who produced 'conclusive

ABOVE The hydro-electric plant at Vemork, Norway, where deuterium oxide (heavy water) was produced for Germany's A-bomb project.

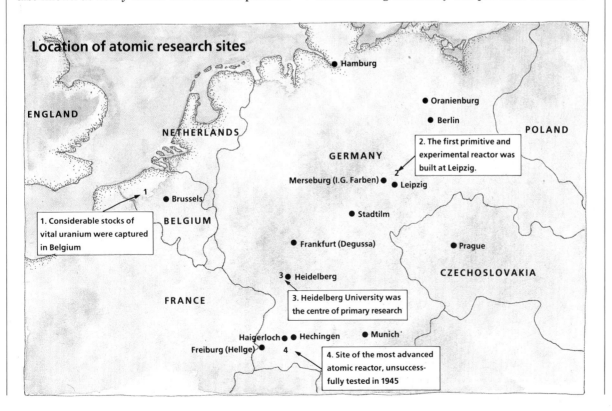

Location of atomic research sites

- Hamburg
- Oranienburg
- Berlin

ENGLAND

NETHERLANDS

GERMANY

POLAND

2. The first primitive and experimental reactor was built at Leipzig.

Merseburg (I.G. Farben) ● ● Leipzig

- Brussels

BELGIUM

1. Considerable stocks of vital uranium were captured in Belgium

● Stadtilm

● Frankfurt (Degussa)

● Prague

CZECHOSLOVAKIA

3 ● Heidelberg

FRANCE

3. Heidelberg University was the centre of primary research

Haigerloch ● ● Hechingen   ● Munich

Freiburg (Hellge) ●   ● 4

4. Site of the most advanced atomic reactor, unsuccessfully tested in 1945

OPPOSITE LEFT The Germans might have been first . . .

LEFT The German nuclear effort in 1944 – the locations of the main research and industrial work on atomic energy in the last months of the war.

BOTTOM The Norwegian factory under Allied air attack, November, 1943.

BELOW Several German factories involved in atomic research were destroyed by RAF night bombers, causing further set backs in the plans to produce an atom bomb.

evidence' to show that it would not work. So they turned to heavy water instead – and suffered a major setback when the factory at Vemork was sabotaged by a gallant band of Norwegian commandos early in 1943.

The faulty assessment of the Heidelberg professor, whose name was Bothe, was made in 1940. Two years later, on the other side of the Atlantic, the Italian physicist Enrico Fermi supervised the world's first nuclear reaction in Chicago – and the moderator used in the reactor was graphite.

In Germany, most of the practical nuclear research work was carried out at the Kaiser Wilhelm Institute in Berlin, or in Leipzig where there was a large scientific institute. It was in Leipzig that the first German atomic reactor was built, and experiments were well under way by May, 1942. The reactor was primitive and experimental, and was designed to enable the scientists to make measurements that would lead to the construction of a workable machine in which nuclear fission would take place.

By this time, key members of the German military establishment, without fully realizing the problems involved, had become convinced that an operational atomic bomb could be produced quickly, perhaps by the end of 1942. The scientists, when pressed to make a prediction, had indicated that an atomic weapon would be bulky, weighing perhaps five or six tons and having a length of up to 24 ft. A sizeable aircraft would be needed to carry it.

At that time, the two biggest bombers in *Luftwaffe* service were the Focke-Wulf Kondor and the Heinkel 177. The Kondor was used mainly for long-range reconnaissance and did not have a very large bomb-carrying capacity, and so the He-177 was selected. In the summer of 1942, one of these

for an increase in funds were flatly rejected. In addition, all German scientific research work underwent a major reshuffle in 1942, and the atomic project came to a virtual standstill while this was going on.

Up to this time, the German scientists had, in some respects, been ahead of the Allies in atomic research. Now the lead had been thrown away, and with America now channelling her huge economic and industrial resources into the production of an atomic bomb, German research was left trailing miserably behind.

LEFT Enrico Fermi. Unlike Germany's scientists, Fermi was successful in nuclear fission experiments and achieved the world's first sustained nuclear reaction in 1942.

BELOW The ferry used to ship heavy water consignments from the Norwegian factory.

aircraft was flown to the Letov aircraft factory at Prague, Czechoslovakia, where its wings were removed and work began on expanding its bomb bay.

Fortunately for the rest of the world, the military authorities had overestimated their scientists' capabilities, and the efficiency of their equipment. In June, 1942 the uranium reactor at Leipzig exploded, causing a further serious setback. Apart from this, Germany's cities were now coming under increasingly heavy air attack from the night bombers of the RAF; several factories involved in the atomic research project were therefore destroyed or damaged.

But the biggest drawback of all was that there was no centralized direction of the project. There was no decision to provide full-scale government support for the nuclear programme, and requests

By early 1944 there were 10 centres – factories and laboratories – involved in the German atomic project, scattered across the country from Hamburg in the north to Munich in the south. By this time Germany's cities were being subjected to a round-the-clock onslaught by the RAF and the USAF, so it was decided to concentrate the nuclear research effort in the area around Stuttgart. The ancient city was not a strategic target, and the Allied air forces had left it alone.

The Germans had so far been thwarted in their efforts to produce a nuclear reaction, but now they set about building a more advanced atomic reactor

BELOW The German military establishment was confident that an atomic bomb would be operational by 1942. The Heinkel 177 was elected to carry it.

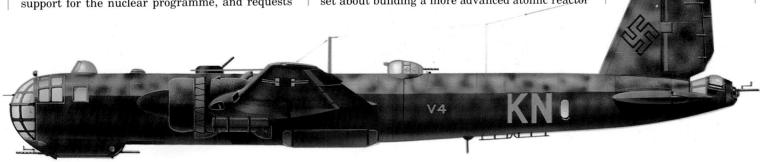

RIGHT Knut Haukelid, the gallant Norwegian who destroyed the ferry.

BELOW CENTRE The cave at Haigerloch in Swabia, where Germany's last atomic experiments took place.

ABOVE CENTRE Dazed, injured and bewildered people in Hiroshima after the atomic explosion. The scene might have taken place in London or New York . . .

OPPOSITE, FAR RIGHT Devastated Hiroshima, 1945.

BELOW The Haigerloch Uranium pile, 1945. The experiment to produce a sustained nuclear reaction failed.

would produce a sustained atomic reaction. The scientists were unaware that Fermi had already achieved this in 1942; they firmly believed that they would be the first to make the breakthrough.

Strings of uranium cubes were lowered into the reactor vessel, and a large alloy lid was bolted into place. A neutron source was introduced at the reactor's centre, and priceless heavy water was slowly poured in while measurements of neutron activity were taken at various distances from the core of the reactor.

The experiment failed, and there was never to be another one. In March, the Allies crossed the Rhine; in the east, the Russian armies plunged on to the Oder. Conditions throughout Germany were now chaotic.

There was little the scientists could do now but wait for the inevitable end. On 23 April, 1945,

in an enlarged wine cellar hewn out of a cliff face in the Swabian village of Haigerloch. The site lay in a narrow, cramped valley between two precipitous heights; no bomber could get at it.

By the end of February, 1945 – with the Allied armies already advancing rapidly on Germany from east and west – the reactor at Haigerloch was ready for the big experiment which, it was hoped,

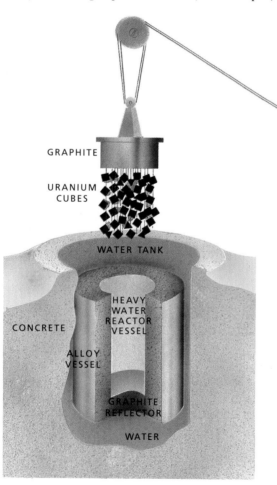

GRAPHITE

URANIUM CUBES

WATER TANK

HEAVY WATER REACTOR VESSEL

CONCRETE

ALLOY VESSEL

GRAPHITE REFLECTOR

WATER

American troops entered Haigerloch. They were accompanied by a special mission whose task it was to round up the German scientists and to ship all documents and equipment connected with the atomic project back to the United States.

At Prague, the He-177, still minus its wings and badly damaged in an air raid, sat forlornly on its airfield, a silent monument to the nuclear mission that never was.

But the fearsome thought lingers that it might have taken place, if the right decisions had been taken as early as 1942.

Adolf Hitler did not live to see the awesome application of the world's first atomic bombs. But the ultimate irony must surely be that they were perfected, in the main, by men who had been driven from their homes in Europe by a pre-war tide of anti-Semitism.

The Fate of Martin Bormann

or many years after the end of World War Two, huge rewards were offered by both the Federal German government and Jewish organizations dedicated to tracking down Nazi war criminals for information that would lead to the capture and trial of one of the men who had been closest to Adolf Hitler. His name was Martin Bormann.

The son of a professional soldier, Bormann was born on 17 June, 1900. After attending agricultural college in Mecklenburg, he became manager of an estate near Berlin. At the age of 20 he joined an anti-Jewish group, and seven years later, as Hitler was rising rapidly to power, he became an active and fanatical member of the Nazi party.

A short, thickset, round-shouldered man, Bormann burrowed ceaselessly like a mole in the Nazi party, furthering his own intrigues and ambitions. He became chief of staff to Rudolf Hess, the Deputy Führer, and when Hess defected to Britain in May, 1941 Bormann was appointed head of the party chancellery. In 1943, he reached the all-powerful position of secretary and chief adviser to Hitler himself.

As Hitler's accomplice and close confidant, Bormann was at the very heart of the appalling excesses and cruelties of the Nazis. Between 1939 and 1942, while still Hess's chief of staff, he collaborated in the mass murder of at least 100,000 'undesirables' – the inmates of mental institutions and concentration camps. Between 1941 and 1945, according to the official statement issued by the public prosecutor of the State of Hesse, he actively collaborated in the extermination of Jews, Poles, Czechs and Russian prisoners of war, all of whom the Nazis considered to be racially inferior. In this

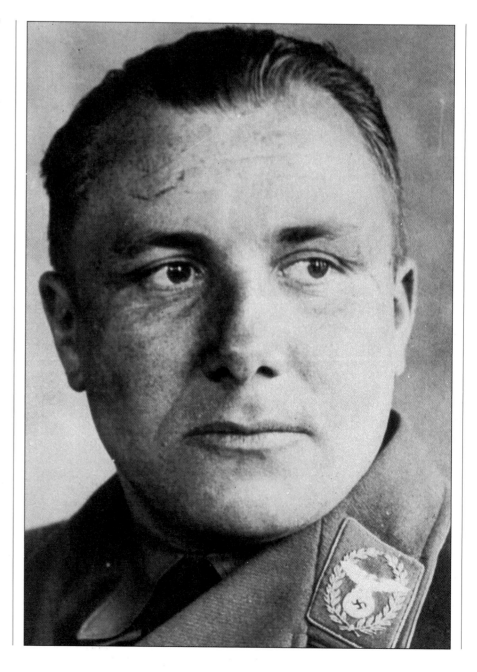

way, the statement adds, Bormann 'with premed-
itation, for malicious, cruel and abject motives,
killed at least five million people'.

In April, 1945, Martin Bormann was one of the
dwindling group of faithful acolytes who resolved
to remain with Hitler to the bitter end. Berlin was
a nightmare place of death, fire and destruction,
completely surrounded by Russian forces who were
doggedly fighting their way through to the city
centre. When Hitler committed suicide on 30 April,
Bormann and Josef Goebbels, the Propaganda
Minister, were the only members of the Nazi 'old
guard' still left in the *Führerbunker.*

Goebbels chose to die, together with his entire
family, but suicide was a long way from Bormann's
thoughts. His plan was to get out of doomed Berlin,
and he saw two possibilities. The first was to send
General Krebs, the Chief of Staff, to the Russian
General Chuikov with an offer to surrender the
Reichs Chancellery if its occupants were allowed
free passage from Berlin. But Chuikov was adamant; he would be satisfied with nothing less than
the unconditional surrender of the Chancellery
and everyone in it.

The second possibility was to break through the
encircling Russians under cover of darkness and
somehow reach Schleswig-Holstein, where German
forces were still holding out under Grand Admiral
Karl Dönitz, whom Hitler had named as his
successor.

At 4.30 on the afternoon of 1 May, 1945, Bormann assembled the inmates of the *Führerbunker* and told them of his escape plan. Most of them thought it was a crazy scheme, but others agreed to go along with it. A little while later, with shells bursting all around and the sky over Berlin thick with the smoke of battle, Bormann addressed a group of SS leaders in the Chancellery garden and gave orders for the disbanding of the so-called Werewolves, the resistance fighters who were supposed to spread havoc among the occupying Allied armies after Germany's collapse. An eye witness, radio commentator Hans Fritsche, noted that Bormann was wearing a field-grey uniform with the rank insignia of an SS general.

At 8.00 pm, those inmates of Hitler's bunker who had agreed to try and break through the Russian lines stole out of the Chancellery. As well as Bormann, the group included State Secretary Naumann, Hitler Youth leader Artur Axmann, Hitler's driver Erich Kempka, and the SS surgeon Dr Stumpfegger.

They made their way through the rubble and eventually reached the Weidendamm Bridge, which crossed the river Spree. Bormann had apparently arranged for them to cross the river under the cover of several tanks belonging to one of the SS armoured units that was still fighting fanatically.

What happened next was the subject of two conflicting testimonies given later at the Nuremberg War Crimes Tribunal by two members of Bormann's escape group. The first was given by Kempka, Hitler's chauffeur.

'Several tanks came along, followed by some armoured personnel carriers. The tanks broke through the road-block on the bridge. Bormann was just behind the leading tank, which became a target. It was hit by an anti-tank rocket fired from a window and blew up. Where Martin Bormann had been there was now just a ball of flame. I myself was thrown to the ground by the explosion and lost consciousness. When I came to, I couldn't see anything.'

Kempka testified that he had seen Bormann's body crumple in the flames. In his opinion, there was no possibility that Bormann might have survived.

But this was not the only version of Bormann's fate. The other witness, Artur Axmann, told a different story.

'The ammunition-laden Tiger tank exploded. The blast-wave hurled me a considerable distance. I instinctively took refuge in a bomb crater. So did several others. Bormann was there, together with Hitler's surgeon Dr Stumpfegger, State Secretary Dr Naumann, Schwägermann (Goebbels' adjutant) and my own adjutant, Weltzin. They were all uninjured. We sat in the bomb crater and tried to work out the best way of getting out of Berlin.'

The group went back to the Friedrichstrasse railway station, climbed on to the track and crossed the Spree in the darkness by way of the railway bridge. After a while they reached the Lehrter station, which was already occupied by Soviet troops. When Bormann and the others climbed up on to the platform, they walked right into the middle of a Russian patrol.

'We had already torn off our rank badges', Axmann said. 'The Russians challenged us and almost certainly took us for *Volkssturms* [German home guard]. They offered us cigarettes. Suddenly, Bormann broke away and ran off towards the Invalidenstrasse, together with Dr Stumpfegger. The Russians grew agitated and we saw the danger that they might arrest us. Slowly, we edged away from them.'

The Russians made no attempt to follow Axmann and his companions – Naumann, Schwägermann and Weltzin – who continued along the Invalidenstrasse towards the Moabit district. Naumann and Schwägermann suddenly disappeared into some bushes; Axmann and his adjutant went on alone, but turned back when they heard the rattle of tank tracks up ahead.

ABOVE Russian tanks advance into the heart of Berlin.

LEFT Berlin, 1945 – this was the legacy of the Nazi regime.

'On the return journey through the Invalidenstrasse,' Axmann reported, 'we came under heavy fire. Shortly after we crossed the tracks at the Lehrter station we saw two men lying on the ground. We knelt beside them to see if we could help them. They were Martin Bormann and Dr Stumpfegger. A mistake was out of the question; we could clearly see their faces. They lay on their backs, with arms and legs outstretched.

'I touched Bormann; there was no reaction. I bent over him and found no evidence of breathing. There was no sign of wounds or blood. Perhaps they had taken poison. Suddenly we came under heavy rifle fire, and had to go on.'

Axmann's testimony was open to doubt, not least because he had been a prominent member of the Nazi party, and since his adjutant Weltzin died later in a Russian prison camp, there was no one to corroborate it.

At a much later date, a number of civilian witnesses came forward to testify that they had seen the two bodies, and that they had been buried. The date of the burial was given as 8 May. One of the bodies *was* positively identified as that of Dr Stumpfegger through identity documents found on it, and in fact the Berlin postal authorities communicated the news of his death to his widow in August, 1945.

But there was nothing to indicate the identify of the other dead man, and none of the witnesses had recognized him. For some time after the war attempts were made to locate the exact burial place, but it was a virtual impossibility; the landscape of post-war Berlin, rising from its ruined shell, had altered dramatically.

BELOW LEFT Soviet troops raise the Red Banner on the shattered Reichstag building.

BELOW Rumours still persist that Martin Bormann lives.

BELOW RIGHT Actress Manja Behrens was Bormann's close companion. She steadfastly refused to confirm or deny that he died in Berlin.

Meanwhile, Martin Bormann was tried in his absence at Nuremberg and sentenced to death. As the years went by, reports cropped up continually that he had been sighted in various South American countries. Most were nothing but wild rumours, but one man who remained firmly convinced that Bormann had survived was Simon Wiesenthal, former head of the Jewish Documentation Centre in Vienna.

According to Wiesenthal, Bormann had sought refuge in Paraguay, where he had several hideouts. One of them, it was claimed, was in the southeast of the country near the Parana River, from where Bormann could quickly escape into Argentina or Brazil if he should be threatened.

With the passage of time, the authorities began to lose interest in Martin Bormann, and in 1973 the West German government officially declared him dead. Their decision seemed to be justified when, some years later, excavation work in Berlin turned up some skull and bone fragments which were checked against dental records and *tentatively* identified as Bormann's.

Despite this, a question mark will always hang over the Bormann case. Perhaps, despite all the evidence to the contrary, he really was the big fish that got away.

Disaster in Bombay

arly in 1944, although the tide of war was beginning to turn decisively against the Japanese Empire in the Pacific, Japanese forces still remained in control of the whole of Burma and were now planning a major push that would take them across the Indian frontier. If they succeeded in defeating the Allies, there would be little to stop their armies expanding across the fertile plains of Bengal, with the port of Calcutta as an early prize.

The Japanese attack, which began in February, 1944, had the initial aim of capturing Imphal and Kohima, in the foothills of Assam, their calculation being that the onset of the monsoon would prevent any effective Allied counter-attacks. The initial onslaught drew six British divisions into battle and bitter fighting developed. Although the Japanese offensive was checked, the situation was critical for several weeks.

During this crucial phase, the British relied heavily on a continuing flow of supplies through the vital port of Bombay, on the west coast of India. Military stores of all kinds would be unloaded from merchant vessels there, then shipped across India by rail or by air.

On Friday, 14 April, 1944, the port of Bombay was crammed with merchant vessels of every description. One of the more recent arrivals was the SS *Fort Stikine*, a 7,142-ton cargo vessel which had left Liverpool seven weeks earlier laden with ammunition, explosives, supplies and aircraft. She also carried gold bullion valued at £2 million, intended to bolster the Indian economy.

At about 1.30 pm, the stevedores who had been unloading the ship's cargo came back to resume work after their lunch break. As they entered the

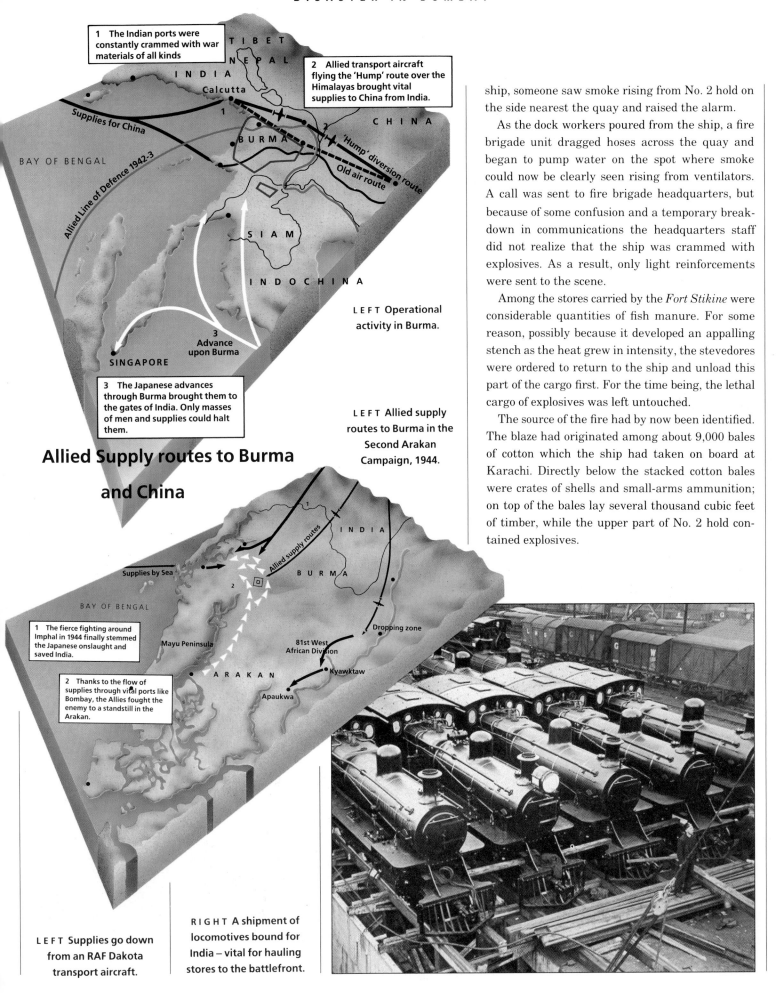

1 The Indian ports were constantly crammed with war materials of all kinds

2 Allied transport aircraft flying the 'Hump' route over the Himalayas brought vital supplies to China from India.

TIBET

NEPAL

INDIA

Calcutta

CHINA

Supplies for China

1

'Hump' diversion route

Old air route

BURMA

BAY OF BENGAL

Allied Line of Defence 1942-3

SIAM

INDOCHINA

LEFT Operational activity in Burma.

3 Advance upon Burma

SINGAPORE

3 The Japanese advances through Burma brought them to the gates of India. Only masses of men and supplies could halt them.

Allied Supply routes to Burma and China

LEFT Allied supply routes to Burma in the Second Arakan Campaign, 1944.

1

Allied supply routes

INDIA

BURMA

Supplies by Sea

BAY OF BENGAL

1 The fierce fighting around Imphal in 1944 finally stemmed the Japanese onslaught and saved India.

Mayu Peninsula

2

Dropping zone

81st West African Division

2 Thanks to the flow of supplies through vital ports like Bombay, the Allies fought the enemy to a standstill in the Arakan.

ARAKAN

Kyawktaw

Apaukwa

LEFT Supplies go down from an RAF Dakota transport aircraft.

RIGHT A shipment of locomotives bound for India – vital for hauling stores to the battlefront.

ship, someone saw smoke rising from No. 2 hold on the side nearest the quay and raised the alarm.

As the dock workers poured from the ship, a fire brigade unit dragged hoses across the quay and began to pump water on the spot where smoke could now be clearly seen rising from ventilators. A call was sent to fire brigade headquarters, but because of some confusion and a temporary breakdown in communications the headquarters staff did not realize that the ship was crammed with explosives. As a result, only light reinforcements were sent to the scene.

Among the stores carried by the *Fort Stikine* were considerable quantities of fish manure. For some reason, possibly because it developed an appalling stench as the heat grew in intensity, the stevedores were ordered to return to the ship and unload this part of the cargo first. For the time being, the lethal cargo of explosives was left untouched.

The source of the fire had by now been identified. The blaze had originated among about 9,000 bales of cotton which the ship had taken on board at Karachi. Directly below the stacked cotton bales were crates of shells and small-arms ammunition; on top of the bales lay several thousand cubic feet of timber, while the upper part of No. 2 hold contained explosives.

flood even the lower portion of No. 2 hold. The only other solution was to take her out to sea and scuttle her there. But this solution would take time to get under way – and time was one thing the fire-fighters did not have.

There followed nearly an hour of indecision and confusion. Stevedores continued the work of unloading the fish manure and other commodities. There was no attempt to evacuate the harbour area; in fact, hardly anyone on the neighbouring ships was aware that the *Fort Stikine* was carrying an explosive cargo. Ships carrying explosives flew a red flag, indicating danger; no such flag was displayed by the *Fort Stikine*.

In one of the ships anchored close by, the Norwegian freighter *Belray*, a young able seaman named Roy Hayward, who had fought fires in the London blitz, saw the flames from the *Fort Stikine* suddenly turn yellowish-brown in colour, and knew what it meant. Burning explosives caused that colour. He shouted a warning and threw himself down in his ship's gun position.

Moments later a pillar of flame burst from the *Fort Stikine*, accompanied by a terrific explosion. The force of the blast was channelled horizontally through the ship's side, sweeping across the quay to obliterate the sheds and warehouses on the landward side. Jagged fragments of metal scythed outwards like a blast from a huge shotgun, cutting down anything in their path.

It was now nearly an hour since the fire had first been detected, and at last fire brigade headquarters had been made aware that they were dealing with what amounted to a floating bomb. All available pumps were rushed to the scene, but by this time the fire was getting out of control.

An army ordnance officer went below and inspected the explosive cargo. He returned, grim faced, and reported to the master of the ship, Captain A. J. Naismith. His recommendation was that the *Fort Stikine* should be scuttled immediately.

There was, however, a problem. The distance between the keel of the cargo vessel and the bottom of the harbour was only 4 ft. Even if her crew did scuttle her, she would not take on enough water to

ABOVE One reluctant passenger destined for the battlefront!

BELOW Loading a jeep on to a Dakota. The Bombay disaster caused serious disruption to the flow of war material for a time.

LEFT Troops boarding a Dakota to reinforce the Imphal garrison.

ABOVE An RAF Dakota.

BELOW Fighting in the Arakan.

Captain Naismith was standing on the quay, conferring with his chief officer, when the blast came. Neither man was seen again; they simply disappeared. A third man who had been standing with them, a marine surveyor from the Bombay office of Lloyd's, had every shred of clothing stripped away by the explosion; miraculously, he was otherwise unhurt.

On the stricken freighter, the explosion killed 66 firemen outright and injured 83 others.

The vessel moored immediately astern of the *Fort Stikine* was the 5,000-ton *Japalanda*. A great wave created by the explosion lifted her bow 60 ft out of the water. The ship pirouetted like a toy and her bow crashed down on one of the dockside buildings.

Flying metal and debris from the *Fort Stikine* caused appalling casualties on other nearby ships, including the *Belray*. Roy Hayward, dazed but unhurt, picked himself up and at once plunged into rescue work, helping the injured on to the quayside, where they were put into whatever transport was available and sent off to hospital.

As this work was in progress, a second explosion, much bigger than the first, tore through the shattered *Fort Stikine*. A huge column of flame and smoke shot up to a height of several thousand feet, flinging tons of metal – including gold bars – into the harbour area and the adjacent town. Flaming cotton, sulphur and resin cascaded into warehouses and residential homes over a radius of more than half a mile, setting them aflame, so that the docks were ringed with fire.

The head of Bombay's fire brigade, Norman Coombs, acted with great calmness and efficiency in the midst of the holocaust. He ordered the military forces in Bombay to deal with the carnage in the harbour area while his own firemen tackled the scattered fires in the town.

In St George's Hospital, 250 victims required surgery, while nearly 200 more were treated for less serious injuries. No one was ever able to establish the final death toll, as many victims simply disappeared in the explosions. Some sources put it as high as 1,200.

For days, thousands of soldiers, sailors and airmen laboured to remove explosives to places of safety from the shattered docks area. In doing so their own lives were at serious risk, for ammunition was constantly exploding in the remains of blazing warehouses. Sixteen more ships, many of them containing explosive cargoes, were towed out into the open sea during the night and the next day.

The cost was frightful in terms of material damage. No fewer than 27 ships had been sunk, destroyed by fire or severely damaged, and all the

dock buildings had been devastated. Three swing bridges at the entrance to the docks had been partly torn from their seatings and leaned at drunken angles. It would take some 10,000 British and Indian servicemen and civilians six months to clear away the wreckage and get the harbour serviceable and in working order again.

In the meantime, the destruction at Bombay was one of the war's most closely guarded secrets. It was not until years after the war that details of the

ABOVE Indian soldiers in the Arakan in RIH Landing craft.

RIGHT A Dakota laden with vital supplies, brought in by sea, prepares to make an air drop to Allied forces at Imphal.

devastation were released by official sources, and then only in a very guarded manner.

During the lengthy inquiry into the disaster, the exact cause of the fire aboard the *Fort Stikine* was never established, although sabotage was strongly suspected. There were a number of pro-Japanese factions in India at that time, and with the Japanese army knocking on India's back door the British authorities had to contend with growing civil unrest, not to mention active interference with the war effort.

As it turned out, the Japanese offensive into northeast India was a disaster. When the Japanese refused to admit defeat at Imphal and Kohima and withdrew into Burma, their army was virtually destroyed during the summer of 1944, paving the way for the Anglo-Indian offensives that would re-capture Burma in the following year.

In 1947, with the British withdrawal from an independent India in progress and the British government anxious to establish continuing good relations with the new Indian administration, in-quiries into the cause of the mysterious disaster at Bombay were quietly dropped.

ABOVE LEFT AND RIGHT The bitter fighting in the Arakan thwarted Japan's ambition to invade India.

LEFT The Norwegian freighter *Belray* with a load of river barges bound for India.

The Mystery of the Pacific War

On 18 April, 1943, Lockheed P-38 Lightning fighters of the USAF's 339th Pursuit Squadron, operating at extreme range from the island of Guadalcanal, intercepted a Japanese Mitsubishi Betty bomber over Kahili atoll and shot it down in flames, killing all on board, including one very important passenger – Admiral Isoroku Yamamoto, Commander-in-Chief of the Imperial Japanese Navy and supreme commander of all Japanese forces in the Pacific.

Yamamoto, the architect of the attack on Pearl Harbor and the strategist behind Japan's lightning conquests in the early months of the Pacific war, left behind him a riddle that has continued to puzzle historians ever since. Was the planning of the offensives in the Pacific all his own work – or did he rely heavily on strategic war plans proposed by American and British naval experts in the years before the war?

Before attempting to answer that question, it is interesting to examine another aspect of the early Pacific war that had puzzled experts for many years afterwards. When Japanese forces struck in the Pacific, they did so unerringly, armed with an almost uncanny knowledge of the whereabouts of American naval forces and airfields. Some of the information had obviously been supplied by agents, but the majority of the intelligence data could only have been gleaned from extensive air reconnaissance – and yet the Americans had no inkling that such activities had been going on prior to the outbreak of war.

It was only after the war, when Allied experts were able to examine Japanese military archives, that they learned the truth. For months before the Pacific offensive, a secret air unit of the Imperial

ABOVE A Lockheed P–38 shot down the Japanese Mitsubishi 'Betty' Bomber, carrying Admiral Isoroku Yamamoto, the commander of Japanese Forces in the Pacific.

LEFT Admiral Isoroku Yamamoto on the bridge of his flagship, the *Yamato*.

ABOVE The Japanese planned their attack on Pearl Harbor meticulously. Here, planners inspect a detailed model of the US base.

ABOVE RIGHT Brigadier-General D. C. Strother presents the DFC and Silver Star to Captain Lanphier, the leader of the squadron that shot down Yamamoto.

RIGHT The burnt-out wreck of Yamamoto's Betty bomber in the Kahili jungle.

The Conquest of Japan

USSR

CHINESE
REPUBLIC

Limits of Japanese conquests
April 1942

Pearl Harbour **2**

Planned extension

1

AUSTRALIA

3

INDIAN OCEAN

1   The Phillipines. Hector Bywater predicted the great Pacific battles of World War II with amazing accuracy.

2   Pearl Harbour – scene of the Japanese attack, December 7 1941

3   To capture Australia was the ultimate goal of Admiral Yamamoto's grand Pacific strategy.

OPPOSITE US Navy aircraft under fierce air attack at Pearl Harbor.

BELOW Pearl Harbor, 7 December, 1941. The USS *Tennessee* and the USS *West Virginia* ablaze after the attack.

BELOW RIGHT The Japanese struck unerringly – Pearl Harbor under attack.

Japanese Navy had been ranging far and wide, making clandestine flights over American bases and assembling massive photographic coverage.

Designated the 3rd Air Corps, the secret unit had three squadrons totalling 36 long-range Mitsubishi G3M2 Nell reconnaissance bombers. In April, 1941, under strict security, they were assembled at Takao on the island of Formosa. The aircraft were ferried out singly over a period of time from Kisarazu, near Tokyo. They were un-camouflaged and carried no national markings.

On 18 April, 1941 the 3rd Air Corps flew its first mission. This was a round trip of 1,200 miles to photograph the harbour installations, airfield and military barracks at Legaspi, on the southeast tip of Luzon in the Philippines. The aircraft made a successful run over the target at 28,000 ft and was not detected.

On 23 April, 21 G3M2s made a 1,400-mile flight across the ocean to Peleliu airfield in the Palau Islands, east of the Philippines. From there they made clandestine reconnaissance flights over Jolo Island and targets on Mindanao. Later, operating from Truk in the Caroline Islands, they reconnoitred Rabaul.

Then, in June, part of the 3rd Air Corps moved to Tinian and began to make very cautious sorties at maximum altitude – 29,500 ft – over the strategically important island of Guam. In a period of three days the aircraft photographed the whole island in great detail. One of them was apparently spotted,

because the United States government protested that an aircraft, thought to be of Japanese origin, had overflown the island at very high altitude. The Americans gave no hint that they believed it to be a reconnaissance aircraft, and the Japanese naturally denied the incident. Nevertheless, they felt it prudent to bring the secret flights over the Pacific to a halt – although more reconnaissance missions were flown over French Indo-China prior to the Japanese invasion in July, 1941.

After that the 3rd Air Corps disbanded and was re-formed as a fighter unit. By that time it had provided the Japanese naval staff with all the photographic intelligence it needed; Admiral Yamamoto could now go ahead and put his master plan into action.

Yamamoto had two attributes that were rare among the Japanese officer class. The first was that he thoroughly understood the Japanese military mind; the second was that he could speak and read English. In the early 1920s he had been the Japanese naval attaché in Washington, and during that time must have had plenty of opportunity to read books and papers on naval strategy written by Western experts.

One such paper was an extraordinary document entitled *Sea-Power in the Pacific*, written by a British naval correspondent and former intelligence officer named Hector Bywater. Part of it dealt with the pattern a future war in the Pacific might follow, and later events showed the predictions to be extraordinarily accurate. It was first published in London in 1925 and subsequently appeared in several languages, including Japanese, and became recommended reading in the naval staff colleges of the major powers.

Shortly after its first appearance, the paper – or at least the section dealing with the conduct of a future Pacific war – was expanded and updated into a full-length book.

Bywater's hypothetical war in the Pacific begins

ABOVE Hector Bywater foresaw major engagements between US and Japanese fleets. Here, a Japanese destroyer manoeuvres hard under attack.

LEFT He also envisaged the use of carrier-based aircraft.

not with a surprise attack on Pearl Harbor, but with a major engagement between the Japanese and American fleets off the Philippines. Bywater envisaged that the main weaponry used would be naval guns, but he also foresaw the use of carrier-based aircraft. That in itself was not remarkable, because by the mid-1920s the British, Americans and Japanese all had embryo carrier forces, and an effective demonstration of what an aircraft could do to warships had already been made in July, 1921 when a combined force of US army and US navy bombers sank several captured German vessels, including the battleship *Ostfriesland*.

What was remarkable was the accuracy of Bywater's account of the subsequent Japanese attacks on Guam and the Philippines. Guam, he

predicted, would be subjected to an air and naval bombardment, after which Japanese forces would land in a pincer movement on the east and west sides of the island. American forces would not be able to mount an effective resistance and would soon be compelled to surrender. It happened almost exactly like that in December, 1941.

The similarity between Bywater's account of the Japanese invasion of the Philippines and the actual event is truly astonishing. He predicted that the assault would begin with massive air attacks mounted by aircraft from a carrier task force cruising to the west – which it did; this would be followed by a three-pronged invasion, with Japanese forces landing at Lingayen Gulf and Lamon Bay, Luzon, and at Sindangan Bay on Mindanao.

INSET The Americans would eventually reconquer the Pacific.

ABOVE Bywater predicted that island assaults would start with massive air attacks.

The Luzon landings proceeded exactly as Bywater had predicted, the Japanese rolling inland to take Manila from two sides. Only the Sindangan Bay landing was wide of the mark; instead of landing at this spot, on the western side of Mindanao, the Japanese went ashore at Davao Gulf on the south-eastern tip of the island – one of the spots reconnoitred by the 3rd Air Corps' aircraft.

Bywater foresaw how the Americans would eventually reconquer the Pacific with the aid of powerful naval forces, moving relentlessly towards Japan in a series of carefully controlled 'island-hopping' operations. He also envisaged how the Japanese, faced with defeat, would throw every available resource into the battle – including suicide pilots.

The great naval engagement that would finally shatter Japan's dreams of Pacific victory, Bywater wrote, would take place where the war had begun – off the Philippines. Strangely, he failed to appreciate the role of air power in his decisive naval engagement; when it actually happened in 1944, the opposing forces traded blows by means of their carrier air groups, the surface fleets seldom coming within sight of one another.

All in all, it seems that the predictions made by Bywater and the strategy adopted by Yamamoto in the early Pacific campaign are too closely parallel

A B O V E Swordfish torpedo bomber taking off on an air strike.

R I G H T The Italian naval base at Taranto after the Fleet Air Arm's attack. Note wrecked Italian warships surrounded by oil.

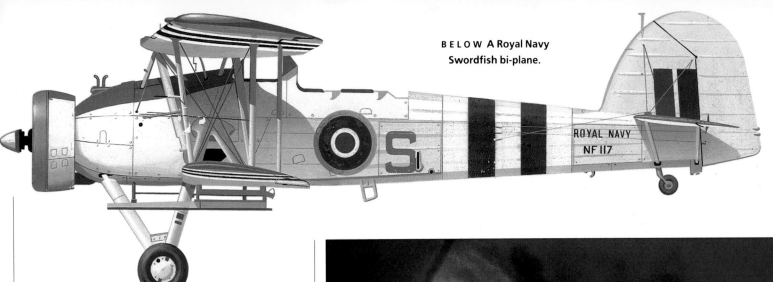

BELOW A Royal Navy Swordfish bi-plane.

ROYAL NAVY
NF 117

to be a coincidence. Bywater had also predicted that torpedo-bombers would be the main type of aircraft used in naval warfare, and in this he was completely correct.

If Yamamoto needed any confirmation of this theory, it was the British who supplied it. In November, 1940, a little over a year before the Japanese attack on Pearl Harbor, 20 torpedo- and bomb-carrying Swordfish biplanes of the Royal Navy swept down on the Italian fleet at Taranto in a brilliantly executed night attack, crippling one of Italy's most modern battleships and two heavy cruisers. The battleship and one of the cruisers were out of action for months; the other cruiser never put to sea again.

The lessons of Taranto were not lost on Yamamoto in planning the attack on Pearl Harbor. Nor were those he derived from widely publicized US navy manoeuvres that took place off Hawaii in 1932, when the Americans themselves showed how it would be possible for a carrier force to approach Pearl Harbor undetected and launch a devastating strike on the base at dawn.

But whether Yamamoto's grand strategy for the Pacific war was based largely on the writings of an obscure Englishman will forever remain one of the war's most intriguing mysteries.

ABOVE The Japanese master stroke – Pearl Harbor in flames after the attack.

LEFT Torpedo bombers would be the main type of aircraft used in naval warfare.

The Fate of Amelia Earhart

f all the mysterious events arising from World War Two, few have excited the public's imagination as much – and given birth to as many wild stories – as the fate of the famous American aviatrix Amelia Earhart and her navigator, Fred Noonan, who disappeared on the final leg of a planned round-the-world flight in July, 1937. Although their disappearance occurred before the outbreak of war, their probable fate at the hands of the Japanese subsequently led to a great deal of wartime speculation.

Flying a twin-engined Lockheed Electra, Earhart and Noonan took off from Lae, New Guinea, at 10.00 am on 2 July, 1937 to fly to Howland Island in mid-Pacific, a distance of 2,556 miles.

Throughout the later stages of the flight the Electra's crew were in constant touch with the US navy cutter *Itasca*, stationed off Howland to provide the aircraft with navigational assistance. At 7.42 am on 3 July – making allowances for the time differences on either side of the International Date Line – the cutter received a radio transmission from Amelia Earhart.

'We must be over you,' she said. 'We cannot see you. Gas running low. We are flying at an altitude of 1,000 ft.'

Sixteen minutes later a further transmission was received. 'We are circling you. We cannot hear you. Go ahead on 7,500, either now or on scheduled time of half-hour.'

The *Itasca*'s radio operator transmitted a direction-finding signal on the arranged frequency of 7,500 kilocycles. The Electra's pilot reported that she was receiving it, but was unable to get a bearing. 'Please take a bearing on us and answer by voice on 3,105,' she requested.

The radio operator sent out voice transmissions at five-minute intervals. At 8.45 am, Amelia Earhart responded. 'We are in line of position 157–337. We are running north and south. We are listening on 6,210 kilocycles.'

That was the last that was heard from her. It was now clear to the crew of the *Itasca* that the Electra was off course and hopelessly lost. Their calculations told them that the aircraft might have sufficient fuel for another three hours of flying; after that, if she failed to make an emergency landing on some other island, Amelia would have no alternative but to ditch in the sea.

The days following the Electra's disappearance saw the biggest sea search in the history of the US navy, led by the *Itasca*, which steamed northwest at top speed to look for the missing aircraft.

Later in the day a US navy Catalina long-range reconnaissance flying-boat was despatched from Pearl Harbor to join the search in the Howland area. The pilot reported that the weather to the north of Howland was bad between 2,000 and 12,000 ft, with snow, sleet, rain and electrical storms. He returned to base the following morning, having sighted nothing.

aircraft flown by Gary Powers had been shot down near Sverdlovsk in the Soviet Union; aerial spy stories were in fashion.

This latest story, which appeared in a biography of Amelia Earhart, alleged that in 1937 an 11-year-old girl called Josephine Blanco was riding down a beach road on her bicycle, taking lunch to a relative who worked at a secret Japanese seaplane base at Tanapag Harbour on the island of Saipan – the Japanese naval headquarters in the Marianas – when suddenly a silver twin-engined aircraft swooped low overhead and ditched in the harbour.

The search, which took in 250,000 square miles of the central Pacific, eventually involved an aircraft carrier, a battleship, four destroyers and a minesweeper, as well as a host of smaller craft. The aircraft carrier – the USS *Lexington* – did not reach the search area until 13 July, having sailed from Santa Barbara, California, but as soon as it did its captain launched 60 aircraft. In the next five days they searched 151,000 square miles of ocean, with no result.

The rumours began to fly even before the search was called off. The whisper was that Earhart and Noonan, their Electra equipped with cameras, had been assigned to stray 'accidentally' off course and overfly the Japanese-held Mariana Islands, which had been mandated to Japan by the 1919 Treaty of Versailles and where a good deal of military construction work was thought to be in progress. Something had gone badly wrong, and the Electra had been shot down by the Japanese, its crew killed or captured.

Fred Noonan was officially declared dead on 26 June, 1938, and Amelia Earhart on 1 January, 1939. The announcement of Amelia's legal death gave rise, perhaps predictably, to a new crop of rumours that she was still alive, and had actually been seen in all sorts of places, from the Caroline Islands to Tokyo.

The same cycle of rumours kept recurring at intervals for the next 23 years. Then, in the summer of 1960, the secret reconnaissance story surfaced again. On 1 May that year, the U-2 reconnaissance

ABOVE LEFT Amelia's Electra at Lae, New Guinea.

ABOVE One of the naval vessels taking part in the search was the aircraft carrier USS *Lexington,* seen here on the left.

When Josephine reached the beach, she found a crowd of natives surrounding two white people, a man and a woman. 'They were both thin and looked very tired', she told a press conference in July, 1960. 'The woman had short-cut hair like a man, and was dressed like a man. The man, I think I remember, had his head hurt in some way.' She said that the Japanese guards who arrived on the scene to arrest the pair told her that they were American fliers, and she later heard a rumour that they had been executed.

At the same press conference, it was announced that the wreckage of the missing Electra might have been found by divers at the bottom of Tanapag Harbour. A generator was produced as evidence, allegedly identified as having come from Amelia's aircraft by her technical adviser, Paul Mantz. When shown to representatives of the Bendix Corporation, which had manufactured generators for the

Electra, however, they categorically denied that it was one of theirs, and said it was a copy made by the Japanese. Everyone, apparently, overlooked the fact that the Japanese used a quantity of licence-built Electras during the war; the generator could have come from any one of these.

Although the claim that Amelia's aircraft had been found was soon dismissed, it sparked off yet another spate of spurious tales. The craziest of the lot was that an Electra which crashed on a mountain in California in 1961 was identical to Amelia's, down to the last detail, even the serial number. The explanation? Several identical Electras had been flown by Earhart and Noonan on

LEFT Amelia and Noonan taking off from Lae. They were never seen again – except perhaps by the Japanese?

BELOW Carrier aircraft took part in the massive air and sea search.

their round-the-world trip, intended to confuse anyone who might be interested in their real mission. (Just how this was to be achieved rather taxes the imagination.)

As to the notion that the Electra *was* on a secret photographic mission, the story falls flat on just about every count. Admittedly, the Electra *could* be fitted with reconnaissance cameras; an aircraft so equipped, and belonging to the British industrialist Sidney Cotton, made a number of secret flights over Germany in the months before the outbreak of the war in Europe. But from the tactical point of view, it makes no sense to suggest that Earhart and Noonan were on this kind of mission.

For one thing, none of the Japanese bases which the Electra's crew were allegedly briefed to photograph was even remotely near the aircraft's planned track. In fact, Saipan, the favourite conjectural target, was nearly 2,000 miles to the north of it. The great circle distance – the shortest route between two points on the Earth's surface – from Saipan to Howland Island is 2,700 miles. Add the two together and you have a distance which would have been far beyond the capability of Amelia's aircraft, even though it had been turned into a flying fuel tank.

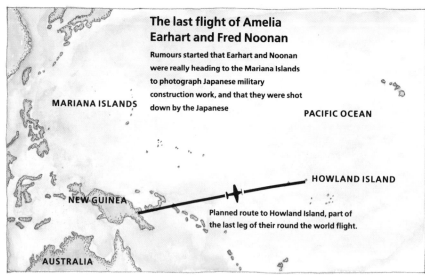

The last flight of Amelia Earhart and Fred Noonan

Rumours started that Earhart and Noonan were really heading to the Mariana Islands to photograph Japanese military construction work, and that they were shot down by the Japanese

MARIANA ISLANDS

PACIFIC OCEAN

HOWLAND ISLAND

NEW GUINEA

Planned route to Howland Island, part of the last leg of their round the world flight.

AUSTRALIA

A B O V E **Was this the last flight of the Electra?**

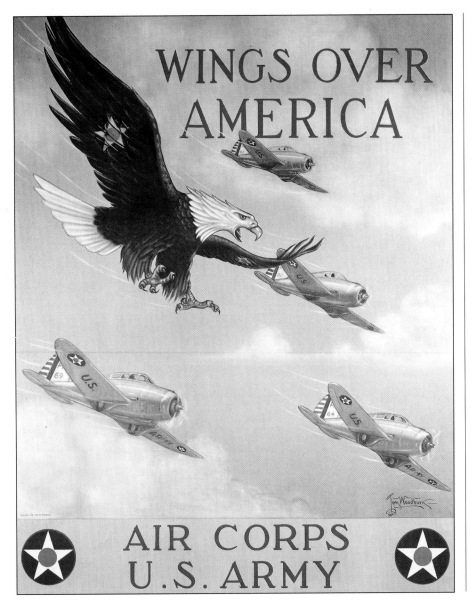

WINGS OVER
AMERICA

AIR CORPS
U.S. ARMY

If the United States government had wished to carry out clandestine overflights of the Marianas – and it should be remembered that in 1937 war with the Japanese Empire was not seen as a serious possibility – it would have been far more logical to deploy a reconnaissance aircraft to a base in the Philippines, or even to Guam, the closest American base to the Japanese possessions.

If Noonan made a navigational error it would have had to be one of appalling magnitude, involving a deviation of some 90° off the required track, if they were to arrive over Japanese-controlled territory. But Noonan was a highly experienced navigator. He would have used astro-navigation to fix the Electra's position at periodic intervals, and even if the weather was poor, it is very unlikely that he would have been unable to see the stars during the entire night flight. A navigational error of such magnitude may be safely discounted.

So what could have happened? The likeliest explanation is that Earhart and Noonan became lost in the final stage of their trans-oceanic flight to Howland Island, began to run short of fuel and were probably forced to descend to low altitude to avoid turbulence associated with electrical storms. They may have picked up the *Itasca*'s direction-finding signals, but in an uncanny parallel with the Liberator bomber 'Lady Be Good', lost in the Libyan Desert six years later, they may already have by-passed the signal's source and been flying away from it.

And so the depths of the Pacific Ocean claimed them. It is time that their ghosts were gently laid to rest.

ABOVE LEFT Parts of the missing Electra's engines were said to have been recovered by the Japanese.

ABOVE A wave of air-mindedness swept through America in the 1930s. It made heroines out of fliers such as Earhart.

FAR LEFT Amelia Earhart pictured with British aviatrix Amy Johnson in 1933.

RIGHT Interest in the Earhart story surfaced again in 1960, when CIA pilot Gary Powers' U-2 spyplane was shot down over Russia.

The Death Train

The Italian village of Balvano, which lies beside a mountain road that twists its way through the province of Campania between the towns of Salerno and Potenza, is picturesque though unremarkable, like dozens of other villages scattered throughout the mountains of southern Italy. The odd thing about it is its cemetery, which is larger than most.

Closer inspection reveals a horrifying fact. The cemetery contains three mass graves, the last resting place of some 600 people. All of them died in mysterious circumstances in the early hours of 3 March, 1944.

Following their landings on the Italian mainland in September, 1943, the Allies, after bitter fighting throughout the winter, had succeeded in driving Field Marshal Kesselring's German forces to a new defensive line halfway up the peninsula. Despite determined efforts the Allies had not yet succeeded in breaking through, and particularly heavy fighting was in progress at a place called Monte Cassino.

In the south, the Allied occupation forces were trying hard to restore order, rebuild communications and ensure a regular flow of foodstuffs and other essential supplies to the Italians, many of whom had been reduced virtually to starvation level during the particularly severe winter. The authorities had to contend with a flourishing black market centred on Naples, where cigarettes and chocolate could be purchased freely from Allied soldiers and then bartered in the countryside for eggs and meat. Consequently, almost every goods train that ran to and from Naples was regularly crammed with hundreds of black marketeers – men, women and children.

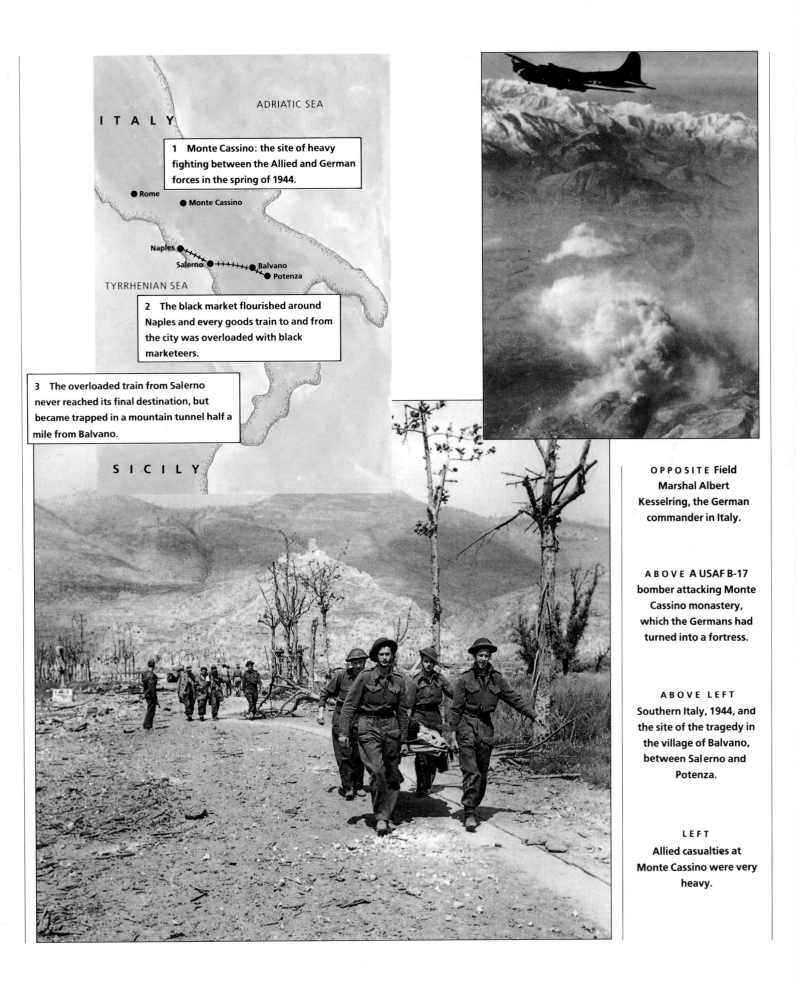

ADRIATIC SEA

ITALY

1   Monte Cassino: the site of heavy fighting between the Allied and German forces in the spring of 1944.

● Rome

● Monte Cassino

Naples ●

Salerno ●

● Balvano

● Potenza

TYRRHENIAN SEA

2   The black market flourished around Naples and every goods train to and from the city was overloaded with black marketeers.

3   The overloaded train from Salerno never reached its final destination, but became trapped in a mountain tunnel half a mile from Balvano.

SICILY

OPPOSITE Field Marshal Albert Kesselring, the German commander in Italy.

ABOVE A USAF B-17 bomber attacking Monte Cassino monastery, which the Germans had turned into a fortress.

ABOVE LEFT Southern Italy, 1944, and the site of the tragedy in the village of Balvano, between Salerno and Potenza.

LEFT Allied casualties at Monte Cassino were very heavy.

RIGHT The Allies go ashore at Salerno.

FAR RIGHT An RAF Baltimore bomber attacking enemy rail communications during the battle for Italy. Tunnels were primary targets.

Getting on to the trains at various places along the line without paying presented few problems. The trains, their locomotives fuelled by low-grade coal that produced only reduced power, moved very slowly along the mountain railways, especially where they hit a gradient. The crowds of black marketeers simply waited at these places, and climbed on. When they were ejected by military police and Italian *carabinieri* at one of the numerous rail halts, they simply moved some distance up the track and scrambled aboard once more when the train was clear of the station.

The goods train that crawled out of Salerno on the evening of 2 March, 1944 consisted of 47 wagons, about 20 of them open box-cars or flat cars. As it rattled on into the mountains, bound for Potenza, it collected the usual cargo of black marketeers, shivering in the wet darkness. By the time it reached Persano, about halfway into its journey, it carried about 600 illegal passengers, together with between 100 and 200 legitimate ones.

High in the mountains at Romagnano, about 30 miles from its journey's end, the train acquired a second locomotive which was attached to the front. After some delay it left Romagnano, churning its way up a steep gradient, but after only four miles it was forced to stop because another locomotive ahead was suffering from mechanical trouble and was blocking the line.

The train came to a halt with half its length inside a long mountain tunnel not far from the village of Balvano. It was nearly three-quarters of an hour before it moved forward again; most of the passengers had not noticed the delay, as they were asleep. By this time it was just a few minutes before 1.00 am.

Balvano rail halt was half a mile beyond the tunnel. The station-master saw the train struggle laboriously past, still moving up a steep gradient, and telegraphed the information to the next station up the line, Bella-Muro. He watched the train disappear into the next tunnel, the mile-long cut through the mountains called the Galleria delle Armi, and went indoors to the warmth of his stove.

The distance between the Balvano rail halt and Bella-Muro was less than five miles – a run of about 20 minutes or so, at the speed the train was moving. But it never arrived. In fact, it never emerged from the far end of the Galleria delle Armi.

At Bella-Muro, the station-master was curious about the non-arrival, but took no action. Even if it had halted for some reason, it would not be causing an obstruction; no more goods trains were due to pass that night. He knew that it was a goods train, and apparently gave no thought to the possibility that it might be choked with passengers.

The station-master at Balvano was also puzzled. His colleague up the line should have telegraphed him to signal the train's safe arrival. No such signal came, but the man took no action.

He only raised the alarm when, shortly after 5 am, a man staggered into the rail halt with the dreadful news that the train was stuck in the tunnel and that most – if not all – of the passengers were dead.

Eventually, a locomotive manned by police and railway officials approached the tunnel. The police went inside and a terrible sight met their eyes. The light of their torches showed dozens of bodies lying beside the tracks. Sickened, they moved them to one side, brought the locomotive into the tunnel and hooked it up to the rearmost wagon. They pulled it back to the rail halt at Balvano, and it was there that the full extent of the horror was revealed.

Every wagon was choked with dead. They appeared to have died peacefully, with no signs of struggle. A few were found to be still alive and

were rushed to hospital in military vehicles that came to the scene of the disaster from Potenza. Most of the survivors had been in the last three wagons, which had been closest to the fresh air outside the long tunnel.

Exactly what happened inside that tunnel will never be known, for the drivers and footplatemen of both locomotives lost their lives. Most of the survivors – their number was never precisely established, because many of them, fearful of prosecution, melted away once they were sufficiently recovered – had little or no recollection of the incident, although one or two believed that the train had slid backwards for some distance.

The likeliest explanation of the catastrophe was that, around the middle of the tunnel, the locomotives were no longer able to develop sufficient power to pull the overloaded wagons and began to lose traction, causing the whole assembly to slide backwards. It was at this point that conflicting actions by the two drivers effectively sealed the fate of the hundreds of people on board.

When railway investigators first climbed on to the locomotives while they were still in the tunnel, they found an extraordinary thing. Whereas the leading locomotive's controls were set in reverse, and its brakes off, the second one had its brakes fully on and its throttle set full ahead. The two drivers, each with his own idea of how to extricate the train from its predicament, had acted indepen-

BELOW Italy's rugged mountain ranges – such as this one forming a backdrop to two RAF Spitfires – made long rail tunnels unavoidable.

ABOVE British troops
tramp through the
streets of Salerno.

dently, and in doing so had succeeded only in making it completely immobile.

Smoke and toxic gases – mostly carbon monoxide – pouring back down the tunnel had done the rest. Most of the passengers must have died in their sleep, never knowing what was happening to them. The lucky ones were those in the wagons at the lower end of the tunnel, where the air was not yet starved of oxygen; when the fumes reached them they wakened, coughing and fighting for breath, and a few were able to stagger out into the clean air.

The final death toll, which was also never precisely established, was between 500 and 600.

The really curious aspect of this terrible tragedy is that there does not appear to have been a searching inquiry into its cause. Nor were questions asked as to why it had never happened before.

In fact, it had – although neither the Italian nor the Allied authorities were aware of it. Exactly three months earlier, on 3 January, 1944, between 500 and 800 people had died from asphyxiation in the Torro Tunnel, Leon, Spain. The incident was hushed up on the orders of the Spanish dictator, General Franco, and details only began to emerge years after the war.

A similar news blackout was imposed on the Italian train disaster, allegedly for reasons of morale. There may have been a more sinister reason: to protect the unknown officials, who may have been Allied personnel, at the depot responsible for supplying a dangerously low-grade batch of coal to the railways.

After the incident, the Italian railway authorities streamlined the procedure for the movement of trains through the mountain tunnels and imposed new safeguards. For the bereaved families of some 600 people, the measures came too late.

The Leslie Howard Enigma

he Morse code message that came through to the signals station at Whitchurch, Somerset, at 12.54 on the afternoon of 1 June, 1943 was stark in its simplicity, giving no hint of the terror that must have guided the wireless operator's hand.

'From G-AGBB to GKH. Am being attacked by enemy aircraft.'

The desperate message came from a twin-engined Douglas DC-3 airliner, registered with the British Overseas Airways Corporation and on this occasion flown by a crew belonging to KLM, the Royal Dutch Airline. There were four of them – pilot, co-pilot, radio officer and flight engineer – and with them were 13 passengers.

The DC-3 had taken off from Portela, the airport of Lisbon, capital of neutral Portugal, at 9.35 Double British Summer Time on that June morning, bound for BOAC's airfield at Whitchurch. There was nothing unusual about the flight; the DC-3s plied between England, Portugal and Gibraltar on an almost daily basis.

The trips were always hazardous, as they involved flying across the Bay of Biscay, uncomfortably close to the German-occupied airfields in the Bordeaux area. But the airliners were painted pale blue overall, they carried red, white and blue identification stripes on their wings, and their civilian registration markings were painted on them in large, clearly visible letters.

Sometimes the airliners were shadowed by German aircraft, but the latter always turned away when the enemy pilots identified the DC-3s as civilian. Until today . . .

But why had the journey of G-AGBB – Flight 2L272, the airliner bearing the name 'Ibis' on its

OPPOSITE Leslie
Howard: Could his
popularity in British war
films have made him the
real target?

ABOVE DC-3 airliners of
KLM, the Royal Dutch
Airline.

Site of the attack on the 'Ibis'

BAY OF BISCAY

Planned route to England

ENGLAND

Flight path of the 'Ibis'

Site of
the attack

Flight path
of German
fighters

PORTUGAL

•Lisbon

Bordeaux

FRANCE

SPAIN

Location of main map

ABOVE The planned
route of the *Ibis* and
where it was shot down
over the Bay of Biscay.

nose – ended in sudden tragedy somewhere over the Bay of Biscay? There had been no one among the passengers from whose death the enemy might have profited. Or had there?

There had been last-minute changes to the passenger list. Originally there had been 14 names on it, allocated seats in order of priority. At the top of the list came government officials or VIPs whose places were allocated by the British Embassy in Lisbon, followed by passengers who had reached the top of a usually lengthy waiting list, special consideration being given to women with children or children travelling alone.

The last-minute change involved the removal of two passengers, a young boy called Derek Partridge and his nanny, Dora Rowe, from the list. A third passenger, Father A. S. Holmes of the Roman Catholic English College, also left the flight after receiving an urgent message summoning him to the British Embassy.

They were the lucky ones.

The two new passengers who joined the flight were listed as L. Howard and A. Chenhalls. 'L. Howard' was in fact the celebrated British actor Leslie Howard, while the other man was Alfred Chenhalls, who managed Howard's business affairs.

A few minutes after 'Ibis' lifted into the air from Portela in the capable hands of Captain Quirinus Tepas, eight Junkers Ju 88 C-6 long-range fighters also took off from the *Luftwaffe* airfield at Kerlin, to the west of Bordeaux. The Ju 88s belonged to the 5th *Staffel* (Squadron) of *Kampfgeschwader* 40, or

ABOVE Junkers Ju 88

V/KG 40 in its abbreviated form, a unit that had been formed in September, 1942 mainly to combat the operations of RAF Coastal Command against German U-boats in the Bay of Biscay.

V/KG 40 had seen little action until the spring of 1943, but after that there had been frequent skirmishes between the Ju 88s and the Beaufighters and Mosquitoes of the RAF. On this occasion, the eight Junkers that set out from Kerlin under the command of Lieutenant Bellstedt had the task of protecting two U-boats that were returning to base after their Atlantic patrols – or so the official version runs.

The German formation sighted 'Ibis' at 12.45, flying above cloud in clear sunlight, and turned to investigate it. Military transport aircraft such as the USAF's C-47s and the RAF's Dakotas – both variants of the civilian DC-3 – were legitimate tar-

gets, but unlike 'Ibis' they were always camouflaged and bore the insignia of their respective air forces. In the prevailing weather conditions, there is little possibility that Bellstedt and his pilots could have mistaken the pale-blue airliner for one of them.

Nevertheless, Bellstedt closed in on 'Ibis' and opened fire. Five more Ju 88s followed suit. Under the assault the unarmed airliner's fuel tanks burst into flames and it plunged towards the sea below, exploding as it fell. Several bodies were seen to fall from the fuselage as it broke up. Predictably, there were no survivors.

The seemingly unjustified destruction of the airliner created a mystery that remains unsolved to this day. One possible reason was supplied by the then British Prime Minister, Winston Churchill, who mentioned it in Volume IV of his *History of the Second World War* (*The Hinge of Fate*):

LEFT Leslie Howard pictured in the making of the film 'First of the Few', in which he played Reginald Mitchell, designer of the Spitfire.

LEFT In both World Wars, the U-boat arm was the pride of the *Kriegsmarine*. They came close on both occasions to severing Britain's trans atlantic life-line. In the second World War, they had the support of the *Luftwaffe*, striking at convoys within range of its Norwegian and French bases.

LEFT
The Ju 88 was
one of the *Luftwaffe's*
most important bombers
and was responsible for
the destruction of the
'Ibis'.

'Eden [Anthony Eden, the Foreign Secretary] and I flew home together by Gibraltar [following a visit to North Africa]. As my presence in North Africa had been fully reported, the Germans were exceptionally vigilant, and this led to a tragedy which much distressed me. The regular commercial aircraft was about to start from the Lisbon airfield when a thickset man smoking a cigar walked up and was thought to be a passenger upon it. The German agents therefore signalled that I was on board. Although these passengers planes had plied unmolested for many months between Portugal and England, a German war plane was instantly ordered out, and the defenceless aircraft was ruthlessly shot down. Thirteen passengers perished, and among them the well-known British actor Leslie Howard, whose grace and gifts are still preserved for us by the records of the many delightful films in which he took part. The brutality of the Germans was only matched by the stupidity of their agents. It is difficult to understand how anyone could imagine that with all the resources of Great Britain at my disposal I should have booked a passage in an unarmed and unescorted plane from Lisbon and flown home in broad daylight. We of course made a wide loop out by night from Gibraltar into the ocean, and arrived home without incident.'

JU 88

JUNKERS FLUGZEUG- UND -MOTORENWERKE A.-G. DESSAU

Leslie Howard Missing in Plane Shot Down by Nazis
3 WOMEN, 2 CHILDREN AMONG 17 LOST: SEARCH FOR RUBBER BOATS IN ROUGH SEA

CABLES from Lisbon last night confirmed that Mr. Leslie Howard, famous film actor and Brains Trust broadcaster, was among 13 passengers, who included three women and two children, missing in the British Overseas Airways aircraft which was shot down by German planes between Portugal and Britain on Tuesday.

It is now known that the passenger plane was attacked over the Bay of Biscay. Signals from its Dutch crew of four picked up at noon on Tuesday said: "We are being attacked by other planes." Then silence.

It may have been so, but others were of the opinion that Leslie Howard himself may have been the real target. The films he had starred in – and also produced and directed – were of inestimable value to the Allied propaganda machine. For example, he had played the part of the British aircraft designer R. J. Mitchell in the film *The First of the Few*, which related the story of the famous Spitfire fighter that played such an important role in winning the Battle of Britain. There is little doubt that men such as Dr Goebbels, the German propaganda minister, would have liked to see Howard eliminated.

But there is another possibility. Also on the DC-3 was a German Jew, Wilfrid Israel, whose family had owned a department store in Berlin until it had been stripped from them by the Nazis. Under an assumed identity, Israel had returned to Germany many times in the years before the war, assisting other Jewish families to escape.

LEFT
Winston Churchill believed that he had been the Germans' target, and felt the tragedy very deeply.

ABOVE
A Junkers Ju 88. The photograph shows a captured night-fighter version, in British markings, of the aircraft that shot down the DC-3.

In London, he set up the Jewish Refugee Mission, and was blacklisted by the Germans as a British agent. The reason for his visit to Portugal in 1943 was to organize the movement to Palestine of 1,500 Jewish refugees. According to some theories, the Germans believed that Israel was selecting scientists with special knowledge of rocketry and atomic research, and putting them to work for the Allies. It may have been the case, and it is known that some of the personnel who worked on Project Manhattan – the Allied atomic bomb project – were picked by Israel.

The truth will never be learned from German sources, as all *Luftwaffe* operations records were destroyed at the end of the war on the direct orders of Herman Göring, the German air force C-in-C. Only fragmentary summaries remain, and the crews who took part in that fateful mission in June, 1943 are dead, most of them killed before the war's end.

Index

Picture Credits